Cracking Your Congregation's Code

To Paul —

Our dear friend and
colleague in ministry.
With every blessing.
        Richard
        Robert

Richard Southern
and Robert Norton

Cracking Your Congregation's Code

Mapping Your Spiritual DNA
to Create Your Future

JOSSEY-BASS
A Wiley Company
www.josseybass.com

Published by

JOSSEY-BASS
A Wiley Company
989 Market Street
San Francisco, CA 94103-1741

www.josseybass.com

Jossey-Bass books and products are available through most bookstores. To contact Jossey-Bass directly, call (888) 378-2537, fax to (800) 605-2665, or visit our website at www.josseybass.com.

Substantial discounts on bulk quantities of Jossey-Bass books are available to corporations, professional associations, and other organizations. For details and discount information, contact the special sales department at Jossey-Bass.

We at Jossey-Bass strive to use the most environmentally sensitive paper stocks available to us. Our publications are printed on acid-free recycled stock whenever possible, and our paper always meets or exceeds minimum GPO and EPA requirements.

Credits are on p. 208.

Library of Congress Cataloging-in-Publication Data

Southern, Richard, date.
    Cracking your congregation's code: mapping your spiritual DNA to create your future / Richard Southern and Robert Norton.—1st ed.
      p. cm.
    Includes bibliographical references and index.
    ISBN 0-7879-5533-7 (alk. paper)
    1. Church renewal. 2. Church growth. I. Norton, Robert, date. II. Title.
BV600.3 .S68 2001
250—dc21   01-01805

HB Printing   10 9 8 7 6 5 4 3 2 1   FIRST EDITION

Contents

Preface

For more than a decade, scientists have been working on the Human Genome Project to crack the genetic code found in human DNA. Its published findings are so significant that it has been described as the "Book of Life."

For more than a decade, we have been engaged in what might be termed a "spiritual genome project," working with congregations to crack their codes and uncover their "spiritual DNA." We've had the privilege of working with mainstream congregations from twelve denominations, as well as with independent congregations. In the process, we've come to appreciate just how important understanding its spiritual DNA can be to the life of a faith community.

Cracking Your Congregation's Code outlines a model that we've tested and used with hundreds of congregations. It is a process that encourages communities of faith to fully realize God's vision for themselves. Moreover, we feel we've developed a practical approach that details what a congregation can do if it wants to thrive in difficult and uncertain times.

Once a congregation—your congregation—has a clear sense of who it is, why it exists, what it is doing, and where it would like to go, it can then create a strategic map for the future that remains true to that identity even as conditions and needs change.

Almost all congregations want to grow—to be a vibrant expression of faith and community—and to attract new members. From our perspective, congregations don't grow because they fail to take into account the most essential ingredient of good health and growth: their spiritual DNA, those intrinsic characteristics and traits that give each congregation its unique identity. But simply going through a process of discovery isn't enough. This DNA, like that in your body, must be delivered throughout the organism—the body of Christ—your congregation.

In the human body, this is done through the circulatory system, the respiratory system, and others. In the body of Christ, the spiritual DNA is also delivered through systems.

Now, there are many systems in your congregation, but we've identified four key systems that carry, distribute, and circulate the spiritual DNA throughout the living body of the congregation: the welcoming system, the nurturing system, the empowering system, and the serving system. Four interrelated, interdependent, interactive systems that work together to maintain the health and wellness of the congregation. Your spiritual DNA, expressed through these essential systems, can become the basis for congregational renewal, growth, and transformation.

Our purpose in writing this book is to give you a clear, user-friendly, practical method you can use to guide you, the clergy and lay leaders of your congregation, to identify this spiritual DNA, which is found in your values, your mission, and your vision. We've packaged our concepts in a practical, easy-to-follow format. This is not a book relating everything you ought to know about church renewal and growth. It isn't our intention to overwhelm you with information. But we do intend to give you what you need to get started on your own journey of renewal and growth, and to provide you with some practical tools (processes and evaluative surveys) to accomplish that.

We've also laid out what we feel is the best way to proceed. For example, it is our firm conviction that the first step is not to begin working on mission and vision statements. Why? Because a statement of that kind without satisfactory underpinning can be written to justify practically anything. Trust us, we've seen it happen. We feel you should begin by carefully delineating what you stand for, what you hold true in the life of your congregation, and that is found in your core values. Once they have been discerned, then you can go on to mission and vision.

The Structure of the Book

To assist you in this process of renewal and growth, we've structured the book as follows. We begin with an Introduction in which we look at the current situation in mainstream congregations and what the possibilities for renewal and growth are. Then, in three parts, we focus on particular aspects of your congregation's genetic code.

In Part One, we look at the key elements in discovering (or uncovering) your spiritual DNA. Part Two examines the four key systems that deliver the spiritual DNA throughout the faith organism. We've devoted a chapter to each system and included some practical tactics you can use to improve those systems. Part Three deals exclusively with strategic mapping. Here we've offered you an eight-step method that leads through specific processes on how you can identify each component of your spiritual DNA, and then how you can move on to mapping your DNA in such a way as to go in the direction of your dream for the future.

We've decided not to make this book a chronicle of congregations we've worked with, as we don't think that would necessarily be beneficial to your congregation's renewal and growth. After all, what you want to know is what you can do to express your own identity, not simply replicate someone else's. Where we feel that a specific example or tactic is helpful, we mention it in the text. We've taken incidents, experiences, examples, and a lot of learning from over the years, and woven them into the fabric of the text.

How to Use This Book

The temptation, of course, is to jump ahead to Part Three, to the mapping how-to, which is understandable. But that's like trying to come up with answers before you know the question. Jumping into things without some initial exploration has gotten many a congregation into trouble. Look at it this way: it's taken your congregation time to get to where it is right now, and it will take time for it to gear up to go in a new direction. So relax, at least long enough to grasp the essentials we've laid out, look at the processes we suggest, and then go for it.

We've found that the most effective way to use this material is to form a team of leaders (in the text we refer to them as a "vision team") who read and discuss the information in Parts One and Two for the purpose of discerning what's best for you. Once you've discovered that, then you can work together to create your strategic map as described and outlined in Part Three. If you have an itch to fast-track the process anyway, we ask you at least to read the Introduction and Part One before you turn to the strategic mapping section in Part Three.

Scripture Quotations

The majority of the scripture quotations we've cited are from *The Holy Bible: Contemporary English Version*, published by the American Bible Society, 1995. Some citations have been taken from other translations and paraphrases and identified as such in the text. Those sources include *The Living Bible: A Modern Paraphrase* (or TLB; Tyndale House, 1971); *The Message: The New Testament in Contemporary Language* by Eugene H. Peterson (or TM; NavPress, 1993); *The Holy Bible: Revised Standard Version* (or RSV; Thomas Nelson and Sons, 1946 and 1952); *The Holy Bible: New International Version* (or NIV; Zondervan, 1984); and *The Holy Bible*, Authorized or King James Version, (or KJV; Cambridge University Press).

A Note on Notes

This is intended to be a user-friendly book with practical ideas that can be used by most congregations. To facilitate this, we've omitted footnotes in the text. However, the Bibliography and the Resources sections will assist you in locating most of the sources of quotations and of referenced data. The Bibliography also contains additional works that we believe are relevant and helpful in exploring your inner geography.

A Few Personal Thoughts

Renewal and growth, in corporate as well as individual terms, begin with an inner transformation and then manifest outwardly in service. Although this book is about renewing and growing a congregation, our own stories (and perhaps your story) have a parallel. In our stories, transformation happened, growth occurred, and a new future was mapped out. Our paths of renewal and spiritual growth came to fruition in the 1980s after a decade of searching. We had both dropped out, in the 1970s, of the denominations in which we were raised to explore other paths to God. But we found that the Church has a magnetic quality of its own, and individually we began exploring the path back, checking out congregations in various denominations.

In the end, we each were drawn—called by God, we now believe—to All Saints Episcopal Church in Pasadena, California. It was at this church, where Sunday after Sunday, George Regas, who was then rector, issued a hauntingly compelling invitation: "Whoever you are, and wherever you are on your journey of faith, you are welcome in this place." This was an invitation home! It was a distinct call to reengagement and renewal—to a new life in God.

As we look back, we realize that our spiritual odyssey was a form of mapping. We first had to be clear about who we were: spiritual beings having a human experience, with our own values and beliefs. Thus our search drew us inevitably to All Saints, a congregation that shared our values and beliefs. It was there that we received the grounding we needed to map our future, to go in a new direction to get from where we were to where we are now.

The process is similar for congregations.

July 2001   Richard Southern
San Francisco, California   and Robert Norton

*This book is dedicated to three wonderful people
who were there for us in the beginning,
and without whose continued support
and friendship over these years,
our ministry could never have happened:*

Robert Warren Cromey, Marcia Sutton, and Linda D. Wiberg

We are grateful.

The Authors

After a career in education, *Richard Southern* returned to the University of Southern California, where he had earned a B.A. and an M.L.A. in history, to pursue a master's in gerontology. He was awarded a fellowship by the National Institute on Aging and served as national president (student section) of the Gerontological Society. During this period, he began studies that culminated in a Ph.D. from Claremont University, focusing on the impact of conservative evangelical Christians on public policy.

Robert Norton spent his early years in the fold of the Episcopal Church. It was during those years that he developed a lifelong interest in liturgical studies, church history, and the history of *The Book of Common Prayer*. After moving to California and getting a college education (bachelor's and master's in marketing), he became a marketing officer at Security Pacific Bank in Southern California. In the early 1970s he and Richard Southern established Norton Southern Associates, a successful bank marketing agency in Southern California, with Norton as president and Southern as senior consultant.

Because of their combined interests in spirituality, they spent two years creating and presenting major conferences dealing with contemporary spirituality. In the 1980s, they became interested in the factors that contribute to a healthy, growing community of faith, and in exploring why so few American mainstream congregations displayed this kind of health. In search of answers, they began an intensive study of growing congregations.

Finally, in 1990, they joined their expertise with their passion for congregational vitality and established Church Development Systems, a nonprofit ministry that, in the words of its mission statement, "teaches churches how to grow."

Since that time, they have explored their ideas with more than eight hundred congregations, in the United States and Canada, ranging in size from twenty-five in average Sunday attendance to several thousand. They have consulted with individual congregations and with clusters of congregations, worked with the founding pastors of two successful new-start United Methodist congregations, established innovative small-group ministries, conducted seminars and workshops, led clergy and board retreats, and appeared as plenary speakers at denominational and regional conferences.

They have been featured in major U.S. newspapers and in a series in a Tokyo daily. They were interviewed on CBS Radio's "The Osgood File" in a segment titled An Ad Man is Not a Bad Man and featured in a prime-time interview segment about church growth on NBC's KNXT-TV in San Francisco.

They live in the San Francisco Bay area.

Acknowledgments

We want to extend our sincere thanks to the many congregations that have put their confidence and their trust in us and in our work. Too many in number to name, they know who they are, and we are appreciative of the opportunities they gave us to work with them in building the kingdom of God.

An incoming message on our office answering machine changed the direction of our lives and our ministry. It was a call from Sheryl Fullerton, editor of the Religion-in-Practice Series for Jossey-Bass Publishers in San Francisco. We returned Sheryl's call, and her immediate question was, "Have you thought of writing a book about your work?" Like most people, we felt there was a book in us just waiting to be published—if only we had the time to write it, and, if we did write it, to find a publisher. This was a heaven-sent call. Meeting with Sheryl and others from Jossey-Bass encouraged us to move ahead. In spite of our initial feeble efforts, she encouraged us, cajoled us, laid down deadlines, and called us to accountability countless times. Sheryl has been a joy to work with. She's every author's dream editor.

Our developmental editor, Naomi Lucks, is a wonder worker. Naomi sees a manuscript as a garden. She prunes where necessary, encourages new growth, weeds out, and uncovers overlooked thoughts, which she then urges authors to develop further, all the while maintaining the integrity of the text.

Lon Haack, pastor of the Lutheran Church of the Resurrection in Terra Linda, California, is a colleague in ministry and a dear friend. Lon has been a church planter and church grower for most of his ministry. His expertise, practical suggestions, and wisdom were invaluable in this project.

We also wish to acknowledge Corinne Ware and the Alban Institute for permission to use the spirituality test and the Spirituality Wheel illustration.

Special thanks to Carol Clark of CDClark Web Development, Santa Rosa, California, for creating the spiritual DNA helix in Chapter One.

Our thanks to David Owen Ritz, former pastor of the Center for Positive Living, Sarasota, Florida, for permission to quote from his article "Service as Prayer"; to Bruce Bramlett, rector of St. Paul's Episcopal Church, San Rafael, California, for permission to include the congregation's mission statement; to Hampton Deck, pastor of First Presbyterian Church, Vallejo, California, for permission to use the "Doxology" quote from his worship service program.

We are grateful to those who have given permission to quote from their Internet articles: Louis Forney, pastor of King of Kings Lutheran Church, Shelby Township, Michigan, from his article "Organizing to be Mission Focused and Permission Giving," www.elca.org/eteam/resources/missionp.htm; Robert L. Hill, editor of *Covenant Group News*, for an excerpt from "Small Groups in the Free Church," May 10, 1999, www.swuuc.org; Rick Isbell, minister of program, Church Street UMC, Knoxville, Tennessee, for his quote on volunteerism on the congregation's Website, www.churchstreetumc.org/volunteer.html.

We also want to acknowledge some very special people at Jossey-Bass. Sarah Polster, senior editor; Mark Kerr, marketing manager; Jessica Egbert, assistant marketing manager; Andrea Flint and Joanne Clapp Fullagar, production editors; and Chandrika Madhavan, editorial assistant. We are grateful to them for their expertise, guidance, and encouragement during this process.

Introduction
The Possibilities for Renewal and Growth

Many mainstream congregations today are like the tribes of Hebrew scripture wandering lost in the desert without a clear sense of direction. Often off course, these congregations need maps if they are to find their way home. Strategic mapping can be of enormous assistance in the journey, because the territory encountered is often foreign or unknown.

By understanding your authentic healthy identity—your DNA—and through identifying the barriers to expressing that identity, your congregation can renew and grow. Your congregation is a living organism (1 Corinthians 12), and as such it must maintain good health to stay alive. Congregational health is directly dependent on healthy systems; if any one system is operating ineffectively, the congregation can find itself in serious trouble. We believe this so strongly that we use the acronym WelNES (that is, wellness). It's derived from *welcoming, nurturing, empowering,* and *serving;* it is intended to convey the concept that having healthy systems means *wellness* for the congregation.

The mainstream congregation no longer has the luxury of simply waiting for better days, hoping that people will get religion and return to congregational life. It's important to act now, and to act decisively. But before we turn to discerning your spiritual DNA and how to create and maintain healthy and vibrant systems for your congregation, let's begin by looking at the current situation in mainstream church life, and why action is necessary.

Making Renewal and Growth Possible

When we look at the current situation, we must acknowledge that America's historic mainstream Protestant denominations, reflecting society, are in the midst of many dramatic changes. We define as *mainstream* those denominations that have their historic roots both in the Protestant Reformation and in the early American religious experience. They define the center of American Protestant religious life. These denominations have a proud and distinguished past—a heritage of great music, majestic buildings, stately liturgies, and deep reverence for learning. They founded many of the major universities and colleges of our land. Accustomed to having their voices heard in the public arena, they often initiated dialogues on public policy and then provided the nation with the best and brightest leaders to deal with those issues. They reached their greatest height in influence, church planting, and membership during the 1950s and 1960s.

Today, these denominations are faced with serious challenges:

- Ongoing flattening of membership and worship attendance

- Dwindling influence on public policy

- Rising competition from an increasingly secular society

- Increase in the number of conservative religious groups

- Bitter and divisive internal conflict within mainstream church life over such social issues as inclusive language, the role of gays and lesbians in the churches, abortion, and the environment

Writing in the 1999 *Yearbook of American and Canadian Churches*, Gustav Niebuhr points out that although many conservative groups are increasing in number and influence, mainstream churches are not. This has caused cynics to comment that these once powerful denominations are less frontline and falling more onto the sidelines in America's religious life. What's happening? Are people no longer attracted to these congregations because of lessening societal interest in religion and things spiritual?

Not according to Roger Fincke and Rodney Stark, who, in their book *The Churching of America 1776–1990*, say that interest in religion and spirituality is at an all-time high. In fact, they suggest that America is actually more religious today, in terms of membership, than at the dawn of the American Revolution in 1776. Even a casual glance at the shelves in a local bookstore reveals growing interest in religion, inspiration, and self-help. Religious themes are often the focus of magazine articles and feature stories in newspapers. Television, movies, and contemporary music echo this popularity. It is displayed in fashion, sports, our political discourse, and on thousands of Websites dedicated to spiritual and religious topics.

The good news for the mainstream congregation is that we are becoming a society of spiritual seekers. Sociologist of religion Wade Clark Roof points out that "the quest theme" in American culture is large: "for example, re-creation of self, improving health and material gains, openness to new possibilities, and so forth." He also half-jokingly commented to a conference of journalists that the names given to vans and sport utility vehicles in this country "illustrate a searching mood in society: 'Voyager,' 'Explorer,' 'Quest,' 'Expedition,' 'Odyssey,' 'Discovery.'" If a mainstream congregation can identify what draws people to explore greater meaning in their lives, and if it has the willingness and ability to respond by assisting them in that exploration, then it could find this millennium to be a time of extraordinary renewal and growth.

People Need Spirituality and Community

Our experience has shown that people have two basic needs today. The first is a need for spirituality, for some experience of God in their lives. Spirituality is defined as "sensitivity or attachment to religious values." Theologian John Shea says spirituality "is all of life seen from a certain perspective. It is waking, sleeping, dreaming, eating, drinking, working, loving, relaxing, recreating, walking, standing, and breathing." Psychiatrist Gerald May refers to it as the deep values and desires that are at the center of our being. Corinne Ware, professor at the Seminary of the Southwest in Austin, Texas, sees spirituality as connecting with God and with each other. However one chooses to define spirituality, it is evident that there is an enormous surge of interest in it.

The second basic need is for a sense of community, a place to belong. Communities in the past—families, as well as social, religious, and civic groups—were an anchor for people, something that made them feel rooted. But those anchors are no longer holding fast. Families, social and religious institutions, and civic groups are quite different today from what they once were.

We live in a highly fluid society, where many say they feel like nomads wandering in a vast wilderness. They often lead anonymous lives, changing homes, careers, and relationships more frequently than ever before. In the course of their lives, they have between four and seven jobs and live in three or four cities in as many states. Some are involved in one or more marriages or relationships. Yet, in spite of the present fluidity—or perhaps as a result of it—people want to share their life experiences, to tell their stories. They seek to build lasting relationships, and to be in some form of community with others.

A healthy and vital community of faith can meet both of those needs: spirituality and community. It can become an anchor in a time of life's uncertainties. But it must design new strategies to do this effectively.

The Big *If*

Meeting people's needs, and responding to the challenges and shifts of contemporary society in new and creative ways, presents a challenge. Is today's congregation capable of meeting the challenge? Our answer is yes—qualified with a great big *if*. True renewal and growth are only possible if a congregation begins seeing itself as a living organism secure in its identity, capable of knowing where it is headed and how best to get there. This prevents the congregation from becoming, as Paul wrote in Ephesians 4:14, "like winds that toss us around from place to place," even when some new religious, social, cultural, or political problems arise, as they inevitably do. Being true to its unique spiritual DNA keeps a congregation on course.

Thus if the members of a congregation understand who they are and what they are likely to become, they can make strategic decisions about their future that will produce results reflecting health and vitality. These decisions are not those imposed by a committee; rather, they bubble up naturally from deep within the life—the spiritual DNA—of the congregation.

The strategic mapping process assists in bringing about this needed clarity of identity and direction. Mapping is also about learning to anticipate the felt needs of individuals and of the community and to develop ministry activities that meet those needs. The question, then, is not whether renewal and growth are possible, but what the congregation can do today to create a future that enables it to reach the highest potential.

People Come First

When congregational members talk about renewal and growth, they inevitably turn not to their spiritual identity but to what they know best: their programs. After all, programs were the lifeblood of mainstream congregations for decades. So they try their hand at implementing even more programs, or altering the old ones, and maybe doing a little tinkering with the congregational structure, or making a few cosmetic improvements here and there in the name of renewal and for the purpose of growth. It's here that they miss an important point: *people don't come to be involved in programs*. People come because they are looking for an anchor, for a sense of purpose in their lives, for a safe space to share their stories, for a place to be with others. They come looking, as we have stated, for spirituality and community, not for more programs. Asking a mainstream congregation to make this shift from programmatic emphasis to discernment, discovery, and spiritual growth is a tall order, but a shift we have seen made many times.

The focus of this book, as in our work with congregations, is on these important premises that assist people in making this shift:

- The congregation is an organism rather than an organization.

- The key to growth lies in understanding a congregation's unique identity, which is found in its spiritual DNA—specifically, in its values, mission, and vision.

- The primary task of a congregation is to create opportunities for individuals to grow spiritually in community with others.

- These opportunities must be present in the interrelated living systems that promote spiritual health and vitality in the individual and in the congregation.

- Strategic mapping is the flexible and adaptive means by which pathways to the future can be charted, implemented, and monitored.

In the chapters that follow, you'll learn some practical strategies for creating a healthy and growing congregation and bringing it into the future. In Part One, you discern your congregation's spiritual

DNA: identifying your core values, discovering your own unique mission, and creating an exciting vision of the future.

In Part Two, you get your welcoming, nurturing, empowering, and serving systems up and running. You see how strategic mapping is able to detail the ministry activities used in each system and provide information as to how the spiritual DNA is being expressed throughout the organism—your congregation.

Finally, Part Three leads you through the specific steps you can take to assess, develop, and monitor a strategic map for your congregation. In developing this map, you detail those ministry activities you will use as you explore uncharted territory while remaining true to your spiritual DNA. Your strategic map not only gives you directions on how to stay on course but also describes the mechanisms necessary to make course corrections on your journey.

It's Your Decision; Will You Answer Yes?

John 5:2–12 tells the story of an invalid who spent years by the pool at Bethesda, waiting for the exact moment when a healing angel would come down to touch the waters. Meanwhile, he asked for contributions from passersby to maintain himself. Jesus approached the man and asked him, "Do you want to be healed?" Without hesitation, the man said yes, and he was healed.

But suppose he had answered differently. He had grown up with his illness and spent years by the pool. People knew him; he was earning a living, and he was used to his lifestyle. He could have retreated into the safety net and said, "No thanks, I'll stay the way I am." By saying yes to the question, he changed the course of his life.

A mainstream congregation, like the man at the pool, also needs to answer the question, "Do you want to be healed?" Renewal and growth, in all their dimensions, are possible only for those who take Jesus' question seriously.

Is your congregation willing to manifest new health and wholeness by exploring your spiritual identity, by taking a hard look at what you do, and at what you might become? You can easily retreat into the comfort of the known and answer, "No thanks, we'll stay the way we are." Or you can boldly take a step in faith and say yes.

How will you answer?

We believe God is calling congregations—your congregation—to engage in renewal and growth. If you say yes to God's call, you embark on a lifelong journey into areas previously unexplored as you meet the challenges that this new millennium is certain to present.

You may agree that your congregation needs renewal and growth, but you may not know *how* to go about it. This book takes you on a journey of congregational self-discovery and authentic change. It is a book about *process*, not about pat answers. Every congregation is unique, and your response to this process is as particular to you as it is to others. Your answers come from your own unique identity, as other congregations' answers come from theirs.

This book is also a resource that you can return to as you begin to explore ever-new territories on your journey. It is an exciting journey for your congregation, a journey toward making better decisions for the future. It is most certainly a journey of faith.

Let the journey begin!

Cracking Your
Congregation's Code

Part I

Your Congregation's Spiritual Code

The body of Christ has many parts, just as any other body does. . . .
God put our bodies together in such a way that even the parts that
seem the least important are valuable. He did this to make all parts
of the body work together smoothly, with each part caring for the
others. If one part of our body hurts, we hurt all over. If one part
of our body is honored, the whole body will be happy. Together you
are the body of Christ. Each one of you is part of his body.

1 Corinthians 12:12, 24-27

When St. Paul described the Church as a body with Christ as the head, he wasn't simply painting an interesting word picture. He firmly believed that the Church is a living organism, composed of many parts that must work together for the good of the whole. The organic metaphor had such power for him that he used it thirty-seven times in the New Testament.

Paul's metaphor tells us a powerful truth: each and every congregation is a living, functioning organism—unique, just as each person is unique. Think, for a moment, of the complex organization of your own body. Your heart, your brain, your blood, your organs . . . all these diverse parts do their individual jobs, yet all work together for the good of the whole body. This harmony—which requires no conscious input from you—is a wonder. How do all the cells of your body know what to do?

The answer lies in the deoxyribonucleic acid (DNA) that is present in all cells. Encoded within your DNA is your entire genetic blueprint: the history of your ancestors, and the information that tells your cells how to grow, fight infection, reproduce, and live to your highest potential. In the same way, a congregation—as a part of the body of Christ—lives according to the information in its own unique spiritual DNA, which rests at its center. Cracking your congregation's code means understanding what makes up your spiritual DNA.

Between 1977 and 1998, Johannes Schreiter, one of the world's foremost stained glass artists, created eleven windows for the Heiliggeistkirche in Heidelberg, Germany. Using as his overall theme "The Illumined Cosmos," he crafted them to fit the gothic tracery of the old church. One of particular interest is the "Biology Window," completed in 1983. In this window, Schreiter used the DNA helix—"the ladder of life"—as the main design. The living Christ is represented in the borders of blood red glass. The artist intended this as a form of "perceptual art," so that a person standing in the light of these windows would be symbolically immersed in the life and sacrifice of Christ. Schreiter has portrayed the Church in his work as we do in our work, as a living organism.

Your Congregation's Spiritual DNA
Your Unique Identity

In your congregation's DNA is encoded your genetic blueprint: your spiritual heritage, how you grow, how you handle challenges, and how you can fulfill your higher potential to be what God has called you to be. As with the human body, when one of these systems fails, the congregation's health fails. But if a congregation's DNA is healthy—if all systems within the organism are working together for the good of the whole—the congregation grows and prospers. (Exhibit 1.1 illustrates the similarities of the human body and the body of the Church.)

The structure of human DNA looks like a double helix or double-stranded spiral joined by hydrogen bonds.

Similarly, your congregation's double helix is made up of two spiraling strands. In Figure 1.1, one strand represents the mission of your congregation. The other represents your vision. They are bonded together by your values.

How can a congregation ensure that its DNA is healthy? The first step is to understand how spiritual DNA works. The second step is to understand the factors that make up your unique spiritual DNA.

A Tale of Two Churches

Let's first look at how spiritual DNA affected two typical congregations in large urban areas. Let's call them St. Mark's and St. John's. These congregations have much in common: one was founded in

Exhibit 1.1. The Human Body and the Body of the Church

The Human Body	The Body of the Church
The human body is an organism —a living thing.	Your congregation is a living organism.
The body is made up of cells, the basic structural units of life that compose the whole organism.	It is made up of cells, basic structural units (teams, groups, committees, and so on) that compose the whole organism.
Within the cells reside the genetic information necessary to build a living organism.	The genetic information of the entire organism is found in each cell of the congregation.
The genetic information for growth, development, and replication is encoded in the DNA of the cells.	This genetic information—your spiritual DNA—affects your congregation's growth, development, and replication.
The DNA is ultimately expressed throughout the organism by systems organized around specialized functions.	Spiritual DNA is expressed throughout the organism by four key systems organized around specialized functions.
The structure of the DNA looks like a double helix, or double-stranded spiral, connected by hydrogen bonds.	The structure of your spiritual DNA is like a double helix; your mission and vision are connected by your core values.

the late 1940s and the other in the early 1950s, to serve prosperous middle-class communities that grew up in the suburbs of a major city during the population explosion following World War II. Both are members of large, mainstream denominations, with almost identical theological positions and stances on social issues. They share equivalent socioeconomic backgrounds, take great pride in their facilities, and work hard to maintain them.

Along with thousands of other congregations across the country, St. Mark's and St. John's peaked in Sunday attendance in the early 1960s, then leveled off, and began to decline in the 1970s.

Figure 1.1. The Congregation's Double Helix

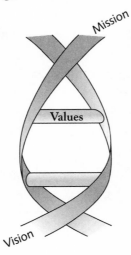

Source: CDClark Web Development, www.cdclark.com.

This decline has continued for more than two decades, even though the population of the surrounding communities has grown. St. Mark's and St. John's were hopeful that somehow the decline would end and new people would be attracted to their congregations.

Similar challenges, opportunities, and advantages—yet here the similarities end. Both congregations made choices about their future according to their spiritual DNA. St. John's decided to retrench along the lines of a model of church that its members knew so well and were comfortable with. So they went through a series of packaged processes, wrote a perfunctory mission statement, and were satisfied with the results. They felt better about themselves as a result of having gone through the process. But in reality, not much happened; not much changed.

St. Mark's took another course of action. When these people realized that the decline was not just an aberration, they took the challenge seriously and examined what they had been doing and asked themselves some hard questions: "Are we reaching out to new people as well as we might? How are we responding to the needs of the larger community? Are our educational programs and workshops getting the desired results? Can we use technology productively? Do our committees accomplish the jobs they set out to do?" In this assessment, they excluded nothing and made no assumptions. More important, they sought to reorganize themselves not by what they'd always done but by their new sense of who they were as a congregation.

Two churches, two approaches. Was one congregation right and the other wrong? Not at all. Each responded to the situation on the basis of its unique identity. St. John's members saw themselves as traditional, and they chose a traditional path. St. Mark's went outside the box of standard methodology in favor of something new and innovative: the path of renewal and growth through strategic mapping.

The Harry Factor

You may recognize something of your own congregation in these examples. You may be struggling to move forward while carrying any one of a number of burdens from the past. In our work, we talk about the "Harry Factor," after this story:

> SMITH TO JONES, SITTING AT THE BAR IN THE CLUB HOUSE: You look terrible.
> JONES: Yeah, it was the darndest thing. We're on the fourth tee. Game's going fine, till Harry steps up to the ball and suffers a massive heart attack.
> SMITH: Oh no! Sounds awful. No wonder you look so shaken.
> JONES: Yeah, and that's not the worst of it. For the rest of the game it's hit the ball and drag Harry, hit the ball and drag Harry. . . .

Many congregations have an abundance of Harrys: problems from the past brought into the present, and often carried into the future. What are your Harrys? Perhaps one of them is a methodology that no longer works, or a desire to hold on to tradition for its own sake, or lack of clarity about core values. It may be uncertainty about your congregation's purpose, or reliance on denominational officials for answers to local problems, or an underlying suspicion of technology and innovation . . . the problems are as varied as the spiritual communities are.

How can you get from where you are to where you want to be without dragging your Harrys into the future? How can your congregation free itself of old baggage and begin to focus on components that produce real renewal and growth: clarity of values, passionate commitment to a purpose, and a compelling vision of what God might be calling the congregation to become in the future? You can do it in three steps:

1. Know your identity.

2. Act from it.

3. Use strategic mapping to chart your future.

Know Your Identity: Your Values, Mission, and Vision

Who are you as a congregation? Dealing with this deceptively simple question requires asking some probing questions. Discovering your identity—your unique spiritual DNA—means first understanding your core values (what you stand for), your mission (your reason for being), and your vision (what you see your congregation being in the future). Let's get acquainted with the terms here and then go into them in detail in Chapter Two.

Core Values: Where Do You Draw the Line?

Core values are the qualities that your congregation feels are intrinsically worthwhile and desirable. Values say what you are willing to do, and where you draw the line. Firmly held core values are so strong that they endure even when the environment changes. They show where your boundaries are; they translate into standards of behavior and expectations.

In the scriptures, God constantly calls the people back to their values. Here's an example. A scholar, quite proficient in Hebrew law, asked Jesus (Matthew 22:35–40) which of the commandments was the most important. Jesus said to him, "Love the Lord your God with all your heart, soul, and mind. This is the first and most important commandment. The second most important commandment is like this one. And it is, 'Love others as much as you love yourself.' All of the Law of Moses and the Books of the Prophets are based on these two commandments." The scholar had called Jesus to reflect on his values, and it is evident from his reply that love was a value. For Jesus, love was the quality that determined his reason for being and his actions in the future.

Core values, as we see in the story about Jesus, are living beliefs. They help you make daily decisions that are consistent with your beliefs. One problem today is that many congregations have lost touch with their values. Quaker philosopher Elton Trueblood observed that much of Western culture (including many of our congregations) has been severed from its roots. He described the results as "cut-flower" institutions. No matter how beautiful cut flowers are at the moment, and no matter how much has been spent on them, and regardless of how gloriously they are arranged, they are, in fact, dead and will eventually wither and decay because they have been cut off from their life source. Without core values, your congregation is as rootless as Trueblood's cut flowers. Without values it is difficult to bring focus to your vision of God's future for your congregation. By living your values daily, you form your character. They are spiritual roots that permit you to flower into a Christ-like life.

Remember: there are no "right" core values. Congregations, like individuals, value different things. As a unique community of individuals, each congregation has its own particular set of values. You work to discover them because they help you sort out what's really important, what you stand for. They impart a clear sense of your principles and priorities; they are a basis on which you can clearly discern your mission.

Mission: What Is Your Reason for Being?

When Jesus said, "I came so that everyone would have life, and have it in its fullest" (John 10:10), he was stating his personal mission— his purpose, his reason for being here.

A mission is a statement of purpose that serves as the organizing principle of all ministry activities. Your activities should be in alignment with your mission. Why? Because it's a waste of your precious resources to do something that does not support your purpose.

The mission of St. Mark's was "to bring the people of our community into a closer relationship with God through worship, education, support, and service." To keep their mission in the forefront of their activities, they restated it in every conceivable circumstance. They printed it in their Sunday program and on their letterhead. They made it into a poster that was mounted around the church. The pastor alluded to it in sermons. Members memorized it and relayed it to others. Most important, they made a commitment to carry it out. That's a true mission.

Vision: What Do You See in Your Future?

Proverbs 29:18 reminds us that "where there is no vision the people perish" (KJV). That is, where there is no dream for the future, life seems purposeless. Your congregation's vision looks ahead to what God is calling you to become as you carry out your core values through your mission.

A truly compelling vision tells a congregation a great deal about itself, who it is as a community of faith, the role of its values, the significance of mission, and the contribution it wishes to make in the world to further the kingdom of God. For example, Jesus often described his vision of the kingdom through parables, short stories that illustrated his point. He would begin by saying "The kingdom of God is like . . ." and then paint word pictures of his vision using the commonplace as an illustration: a mustard seed, a farmer working the fields, a woman making bread, things his average listener could easily comprehend. In the same way, your vision is a picture of your congregation's highest potential, a picture you can all see and understand.

Let's go back to St. Mark's. The members of the congregation identified "innovation" as one of their core values, and in their vision process they explored creative and practical ways to fulfill their mission of communicating the power of the Gospel. What better way than through technology? They fulfilled one aspect of this by investing in a multiuse personal computer with new software programs to develop tools for outreach as well as track attendance, volunteer opportunities, and financial support. The software included PowerPoint, which they used for presentations during worship services and at meetings. Through e-mail, they could transform how they communicate with each other. *Innovation* became more than a word; it was an important part of their vision.

Act from Your Identity: Four Key Systems of the Congregation

In our work, we have found four key systems that have an impact on the health and growth of a congregation: welcoming, nurturing, empowering, and serving. These simple systems profoundly affect both incorporated members and newcomers by permitting entry to, and then deepening of, the spiritual experience. If any of these systems is functioning poorly, or not at all, the congregation founders. When the systems work together effectively, the congregation comes alive and grows. (We take a brief look at each system now and explore them in depth in Chapters Three through Six.)

The Welcoming System

Everyone knows that newcomers want to feel welcomed; but not every congregation knows the best way to accomplish this. The welcoming system is a web of fluid relationships, serving as an entry point for new life into your congregation.

Hebrews 13:2 reminds us to "be sure to welcome strangers into your home. By doing this, some have welcomed angels as guests, without even knowing it." This means working positively to attract newcomers and fostering a safe environment in which all members can explore spirituality and community.

The Nurturing System

Most congregations know that it is easier to get people to come to church than it is to get them to come back. The nurturing system nourishes the new life that has been introduced into the spiritual organism and helps the newcomer feel safe through support groups, classes, workshops, worship opportunities, or mentoring activities. Those who do come back and stay become part of the living body of Christ, "citizens with everyone else who belongs to the family of God" (Ephesians 2:19). They have moved toward discipleship. The health of this system has a great effect on the overall health of the congregation.

The Empowering System

In a healthy body, all the cells do what they are intended to do. The empowering system finds ways to help each person discover his or her spiritual gifts and passions; it supports people in using them for the benefit of the entire congregation. In effect, the empowering system has as its intention that "God's people will be equipped to do better work for him, building up the church, the body of Christ, to a position of strength and maturity" (Ephesians 4:12, TLB). The vision of the priesthood of all believers, the dream that all are called to ministry, is compelling; but it is not a reality in many congregations. Making this system healthier inspires a congregation to take great strides in making the dream real.

The Serving System

Service to others is the most powerful way for an individual to grow spiritually. Service is a way for servant-leaders to emerge. This congregational system is usually embodied in teams and small groups. "If we can serve others," Paul wrote in Romans 12:7–8, "we should serve. If we can teach, we should teach. If we can encourage others, we should encourage them. If we can give, we should be generous. If we are leaders, we should do our best. If we are good to others, we should do it cheerfully."

Ministry Pathways Express DNA

Ministry pathways—programs that take the congregation in the direction of its vision—emerge naturally from strong, healthy systems. A ministry pathway is simply a way of expressing the spiritual DNA of the congregation programmatically. The pathway could be worship, education, children's programming, music, art, and so on. The pathway matches the spiritual DNA of the congregation with the gifts of the congregants.

Strategic Mapping: Charting Your Congregation's Future

Discovering your spiritual DNA clarifies your identity. Making sure your key systems are healthy ensures that you are on a strong path to the future. Strategic mapping gives direction to this future by charting pathways into unexplored territory.

The process of discovering your spiritual DNA inevitably brings up two powerful emotions. On the one hand, it is a tremendously exciting process. On the other hand, the unknown can be somewhat anxiety-producing. Strategic mapping can substantially lessen anxiety by constituting a flexible and open process for staying on course, and it gives the congregation ways to change direction should it run into a major obstacle.

There's an old story—probably apocryphal—of the aircraft carrier whose crew saw an unidentified blip on the radar screen. In one telling of it, from the bridge the admiral shouted out the order, "Tell them to change their course by twenty degrees." The blip sent the reply, "Change *your* course by twenty degrees." The admiral bellowed, "Send this message: 'I'm an admiral! Change *your* course by twenty degrees immediately.'" To his astonishment, the blip replied, "I'm a seaman first class! Change *your* course by twenty degrees, immediately." The admiral was furious. "Send this message. I order you to change your course twenty degrees or risk being hit by an aircraft carrier." After a brief delay, the admiral received this message: "This is a lighthouse. You'd better change your course by twenty degrees."

As the admiral learned, sticking to a predetermined course—as good as it might have been when first planned—is not always the best way to realize your vision. The unique contribution of strategic mapping is that it not only details the congregation's spiritual DNA (how it is delivered, and how to stay on course) but also is a guide the congregation can refer to when its members find themselves facing an unexpected barrier or navigating uncharted waters.

Strategic Mapping Is Flexible

Things move with amazing speed in our often chaotic and rapidly changing postmodern world. A congregation, too, must learn to move just as quickly. Strategic planning and strategic mapping are two good ways to get your congregation from where it is to where it wants to be. However, strategic planning is too often tied to property, program, and hierarchical control. It frequently defines goals, choices, and programs on the basis of linear decisions. Planning is less sensitive to immediate feedback from the environment.

Strategic mapping, which we prefer over strategic planning, is tied to values, mission, vision, and permission-giving. Thus mapping gives a congregation room to make course adjustments as needed because it draws boundaries while leaving open the space *between* the boundaries. In this open space, there is ample room for flexibility and exploration. Mapping is an open and living method for helping you find your way to your vision. It anticipates changing needs by developing a way to meet those needs spontaneously, wherever and whenever they may occur. It is, therefore, both future-focused and committed to comprehending the dynamic forces that shape the congregation. Mapping underscores the necessity of knowing where a congregation is in the present moment, to give it a better chance of getting to its desired future. Mapping defines current reality according to the spiritual DNA of the congregation. It offers new means to create, test, and modify strategic options.

A strategic map is purposely flexible. This flexibility assists the congregation in times of unexpected change, yet it allows the renewal and growth process to remain vital and active. Strategic mapping is a process; a strategic map is a result of the process.

We were invited by the Center for Positive Living, a large congregation in Sarasota, Florida, to consult with them on their renewal and growth. We flew into Miami so we could drive across the state and in so doing visit the Everglades. We planned to travel on Highway 41, which the auto club said is the straightest and fastest route across the state. Our plan was to take Highway 41 all the way. But our planned route did not account for current reality: great stretches of the highway were under construction, which meant slow traffic, interminable delays, and the possibility of being late for our appointment in Sarasota. Clearly, we had to shift to strategic mapping to find an alternate route that would get us to our destination on time. Our vision of being with our client congregation in Sarasota did not change, but our route for getting there certainly did.

Strategic mapping requires thinking and acting outside the box. Rather than focusing on the past—on the Harrys that you are dragging along—this process *intentionally* plots an unexplored future. It understands that decisions made today affect tomorrow, which may mean being open to breaking or reformulating existing rules and procedures. Living in a world of rapid and random change means you must be able to adapt to new situations. A congregation may be willing to be flexible and adaptive but not know how. Strategic mapping is one effective way to accomplish that.

Staying on Course

You may have seen the billboard of the "God Ad" campaign that reads, "Will the Road You Are on Get You to My Place? (signed) God." Answering this question often requires traveling an unfamiliar path. Strategic mapping helps to plot new routes and also helps a congregation regain bearings if it drifts off course. If you recall what happened to *Apollo 11* on its way to the moon, you know how important this is. If you don't, let us refresh your memory.

In the early 1960s, President John F. Kennedy had a vision: he saw a man walking on the moon by the end of the decade. JFK's vision reflected the country's commitment to the values that space exploration embodied. In response, NASA created the Apollo lunar project, with a clear mission to land men on the moon and return them safely to earth. To do this, they had to create new systems. There were innumerable unknowns and great risks; in fact, the scientists were not completely sure they could bring the astronauts back to earth. Since this was the first time such an attempt had been considered, they had no examples to fall back on. They were literally charting new territory.

The launch was successful, but on the journey to the moon the *Apollo 11* spacecraft was off course 97 percent of the time. Fortunately, NASA scientists did not stick stubbornly to their strategic plan; they switched to a strategic mapping mode. Through careful monitoring and intricate corrections, they were able to bring the craft back to its intended course. On July 20, 1969, astronaut Neil Armstrong became the first person to step onto the surface of the moon—and yes, the astronauts were returned safely to earth. Kennedy's vision had become reality. What might the outcome have been if NASA created an inflexible plan and stuck to it, no matter what?

A congregation may find itself in a situation like that of *Apollo 11*. It might simply go into denial and refuse to believe it is off course and so continue the ministry activities that are contributing to the problem. Strategic mapping can help you keep your bearings, move with confidence in the direction of your vision, and make adjustments as needed—all the while remaining faithful to your spiritual DNA.

Scan, Design, and Monitor

In mapping the systems, your congregation intentionally charts its future through three steps: scanning, designing, and monitoring.

Scanning means assessing the current health of your congregation's four key systems. In the scanning step, we examine each system to ascertain if they are in balance or out of balance. Once this has been determined, we move on to designing.

Designing is creating new tactics (the mechanisms for transforming change) that meet the needs of the present moment and strengthen each system. Openness, creativity, and flexibility are imperative for this step if the congregation is to avoid unnecessary detours and pitfalls on its journey. This probably includes designing ministry activities that have not been considered previously.

Monitoring tracks progress. After designing new activities to strengthen the systems, the congregation carefully monitors the changes to determine if they are producing the intended results. If they are not, the congregation can design and implement new modifications and then monitor them to track progress. We look at all of this in detail in Part Three of this book.

A Profound Difference

Abraham Lincoln once wrote, "If we could first know where we are, and where we're going, we could better judge what to do, and how to do it." Lincoln's insight is valuable for any congregation. You must know who you are, and you must know where you are headed. You must also know how to change directions, if necessary, to get back on track. This is the unique contribution of strategically mapping your spiritual DNA. In the next chapter, we get started on this exciting and fulfilling process.

2

Cracking Your Spiritual Code

Growing into Who You Are

There's more to your congregation than meets the eye. Just as the human organism inherits certain genetic traits, characteristics, and dispositions that in combination make up the whole person, so your congregation has a complex inheritance. Many factors, including denominational, liturgical, and cultural inheritance, go into making it what it is. Author Ken Wilber says that "to understand the whole, it is necessary to understand the parts. To understand the parts, it is necessary to understand the whole."

Your Spiritual Inheritance

Nearly two millennia have passed since St. Paul identified the Church as "the body of Christ." He then went beyond metaphor by using the human body as an analogy. Paul wrote, "Our bodies don't have just one part. They have many parts." These parts, he said, cannot act independently. They must work in a harmonious relationship to keep the whole body healthy.

Suppose, he wrote, a foot says, "'I'm not a hand, and so I'm not part of the body.' Wouldn't the foot still belong to the body? Or suppose an ear says, 'I'm not an eye, and so I'm not part of the body.' Wouldn't the ear still belong to the body? If our bodies were only an eye, we couldn't hear a thing. And if they were only an ear, we couldn't smell a thing. But God has put all parts of our body together in the way he decided is best!" (1 Corinthians 12:14–18). Paul was quite clear that the Church—the body of Christ—is a living organism, with specific, identifiable parts that work together for the good of the whole.

Congregations, of course, read Paul's words frequently. But are the words understood as poetic metaphor or as a practical, real-time model for the Church? Evidence indicates that the poetic approach wins out. There is a long history of thinking of the Church as an organization dependent on others for its life, rather than as an organism in which life already exists. This organizational model has become so deeply ingrained that changing it requires a profound shift in consciousness, one that compels us to rethink the very nature of the Church.

Denominational Inheritance

The principles we've described as significant in discerning your congregation's spiritual DNA are applicable to religious traditions. A denomination passes on its own inherited spiritual DNA—those characteristics, beliefs, and cultural features that create a public identity as well as a connecting link to its congregations. Let's highlight a few of the inherited genetic traits of some mainstream denominations.

Lutherans stress the importance of Word and sacrament. The Bible is the written witness of God's revelation. One is saved by grace through faith. Episcopalians, in a theologically diverse Church, uphold the importance of liturgy and the centrality of the Eucharist, as received through *The Book of Common Prayer*. United Methodism is committed to the importance of faith and works, through Christian living and social justice. Presbyterians hold that the true church is where the gospel is truly preached and heard in a community that values stately worship and intellectual achievement. The United Church of Christ's heritage features appreciation for the way God has worked in the past, while recognizing the continuing need for adapting the work of ministry to the needs of our time. The Christian Church (Disciples of Christ) emphasizes Christian unity based on Scripture and has a strong sense of ecumenism. The Reformed Church in America, the oldest Protestant body with uninterrupted ministry, treasures its past, but it has provided innovative ministries through the work of Norman Vincent Peale and Robert Schuller. At the Reformation, Baptists sought restoration of the first-century Church and in doing so stressed individual conscience in the light of Scripture rather than creedal uniformity.

These historic bodies, and those congregations that have grown out of the New Thought movement, do have inherited differences. Yet they have even more in common, in their challenges, strengths, and resources. To map their future, it is important to be aware of the past and, of course, the present.

How Environment Affects Your Spiritual DNA

Spiritual DNA does not exist in a vacuum; nor is it subject only to its own internal heritage. It is also affected by environmental factors. Perhaps there are no longer any children or younger families in the community. The neighborhood has changed, but a congregation's core constituency has not. A congregation assumes that its desired target audience exists in the geographical area, when it fact it does not. Clearly, your environment can affect the growth of a ministry in your congregation, even if the ministry reflects your spiritual DNA. The circumstances and conditions by which you are surrounded *do* make a difference.

Environment can affect your mission and vision in other ways as well. One client congregation felt a strong commitment to serve the physically challenged. This reflected their values, and the congregants saw it as a compelling way to implement their mission; it was in alignment with their spiritual DNA. As they were exploring ways to bring this into reality, it became clear that there was a major environmental impediment. The church architect had placed all the restrooms on the second floor! The congregation did not have the financial resources to build restrooms on the street level, nor did they have funding for an elevator. So they had to be realistic and put their dream on hold; the environment did not support ministry to the disabled at that time.

You *Can* Change Your DNA

Today, scientists are close to being able to monitor, modify, alter, and repair our human genetic makeup. The genetic makeup of the body of Christ can also be modified. Ordination of women is a case in point.

In 1853, Antoinette Louisa Brown was ordained as minister of First Congregational Church in Wayne County, New York. She was the first woman ordained in a mainstream American denomination. By 1893, the Congregationalists had nine women in ordained ministry. Baptists and the Disciples of Christ ordained several women by the mid-nineteenth century. Attainment of women's suffrage in 1920 signaled a new era, but most tradition-bound denominations remained steadfastly opposed to the idea of women in the ordained ministry. By the mid-1950s, however, thinking had changed; and in 1956 Methodists and Presbyterians granted full clergy rights to women. By 1970, two Lutheran bodies authorized women's ordination. Episcopalians began ordaining women to the priesthood and the episcopate in 1977. The old genetic makeup of these denominations was modified and altered. Because new genetic material was introduced, their spiritual DNA has been forever altered.

Spiritual DNA can also be modified by denominational merger. Examples are the formation of the United Church of Christ in 1957, the United Methodist Church in 1968, the Presbyterian Church (USA) in 1983, and the Evangelical Lutheran Church in America in 1988. These mergers moved forward in relative harmony because the spiritual DNA of the bodies involved was compatible. Not all congregations from the participating denominations, though, went along with these historic actions. They asserted that as a result of the merger, they were now the keepers of "the faith once delivered"—

possessors of the true DNA—and they banded together to form "continuing" denominations.

Sometimes, despite apparent similarities, differences run deep. Here's a prime example. The Episcopal Church and the Evangelical Lutheran Church in America have many commonalities. They share historical Reformation links. Their liturgies are similar. They take communion in one another's parishes and celebrate the Eucharist with each other. So closely have they worked and dialogued together for more than thirty years that someone, with tongue in cheek, has suggested that if a merger ever does take place the members might be called "Lutherpalians." Both denominations took a major step forward in 1999–2000 by entering into "full communion" to work closely in common mission, starting new ministries, and supporting struggling congregations. Full communion, however, is not merger. So, why, with such an amicable relationship, don't they form one large denomination?

On the surface it looks fine, but as we have noted, there's more here than meets the eye. There are significant differences in their spiritual DNA, stemming largely from each denomination's understanding of ministry. Episcopalians view the historic episcopate, as it has been passed down from apostolic times, as being a vital and necessary part of their spiritual DNA. Lutheran spiritual DNA is centered in the Word, and power and authority in the Church resides in the Word alone. It is no small matter for either side to alter its identity, and it remains to be seen whether they can modify their DNA sufficiently to eventually become one.

Such is the power of inherited spiritual DNA. Let's turn our attention now to those genetic elements that all congregations, regardless of denominational or environmental inheritance, must understand.

Your Core Values

The first step toward cracking your congregation's code is to agree on your core values: the beliefs that define your very essence as a congregation. Your values show how you respect others, what you hold in highest regard, and what you want to hold on to. They determine how you go about building the kingdom of God.

Values Are Clear, Not Vague

Mainstream congregations tend to be generous in their worldview, in their missional giving, and in their openness to the ideas of others. They are particularly generous in their willingness to go to any length not to offend. They would agree with Philippians 4:8 that we should never "stop thinking about what is truly worthwhile and worthy of praise." Yet when asked to venture past the thinking stage—to be specific and define exactly what is truly worthwhile and worthy of praise—most people tend to get a little vague: "We stand for all values. You name 'em—love, trust, courage, beauty, integrity, and so on—we love 'em all." And they do.

So if a congregation loves 'em all, why specify and define core values? Because there is often a gap between what is held up as a high ideal and what is done in actual practice. In other words, a congregation doesn't always carry out the ideals it espouses. This is not intentional. It is typically the result of lack of clarity as to how the values are implemented through ministry. Lack of clarity inevitably results in wrangling, disagreement, and dissension.

An "honest to God, this really happened" example, we feel, makes the point.

Pastor Jeff led a congregation made up largely of folks of Scandinavian origin who felt very strongly about diversity as a core value of their congregation. They talked extensively about diversity in general terms, though they had never defined it and, as far as the pastor was concerned, didn't truly practice it. When Jeff suggested that they reach out to some of the minority groups in the area, there was mild interest but no specific activity to do so. When a biracial couple attended the church, they were largely ignored.

Jeff was confused. How can the congregation claim to hold diversity as a core value yet not seem willing to practice it? The more he brought up the subject, the deeper the resistance and dissension. He called us in and told us the story. We asked him a simple question: Had the members of the congregation ever defined what they meant by the word? He gave a typical mainstream answer: "Why should we? We know what it means. It's obvious to anybody what diversity means. And if these folks really believed it, we'd see it reflected in the makeup of the congregation on Sunday mornings."

Still we suggested he discuss it openly. He chose his Bible class as a test case. He asked them if they truly believed in diversity. Yes, they replied. He asked if the congregation practiced it? Of course, they said. "Well," he asked them, "where is this diversity? I don't see it." "Why, Pastor," someone said, quite seriously, "look around this group. We are a diverse congregation. We have Norwegians, Danes, and Swedes. That's diversity."

Clarity about what diversity meant came from their discussion. This incident is illustrative of why defining each core value as carefully as possible is worth the effort. (Oh, by the way: Jeff now happily pastors a multiracial congregation that defines diversity in much the same way he does.)

Clear Values Equal Clear Decisions

Your values form the basis for developing policy and procedure, for creating cohesiveness and teamwork, for developing ministry activity that serves the congregation and the community. They help you make proper choices when conflict arises, and they provide strength and guidance in good times and bad. They help you decide where to invest your time, how to act, and on what to concentrate your resources and energy. You move forward on projects that properly promote your core values, and discard those that do not. Core values indicate what you will do, and they also dictate what you should *not* do.

Values vary from congregation to congregation. Your values help attract to you those who share them. Values reflect what you stand for and what you hold to be significant. They communicate to newcomers what they can expect if they join you. Clearly communicated core values foster loyalty and commitment among everyone associated with the congregation.

The number of values you can rack up is not so important as the clarity you bring to those central values around which there is consensus. The values should mirror your current reality, as well as the vision of what the congregation aspires to achieve in the future. They don't have to say everything that is important to the congregation, but they should highlight its unique priorities.

Discerning your core values is a three-step process:

1. *Identify* those three to five values that are an essential part of the life and work of your congregation.

2. *Define*—in writing—exactly what each of these values means in the life of your congregation.

3. *Prioritize* them, because they have varying degrees of importance and meaning in the life of your congregation.

In 1 Corinthians 13, Paul provides an excellent example of this process in his discussion of a particular core value: love. First, he identified its importance with these words: "What if I could speak all languages of humans and of angels? If I did not love others, I would be nothing more than a noisy gong or a clanging cymbal" (v. 1).

Second, he then defined what love is (vv. 4–8): "Love is kind and patient, never jealous, boastful, proud, or rude. Love isn't selfish or quick tempered. It doesn't keep a record of wrongs that others do. Love rejoices in the truth, but not in evil. Love is always supportive, loyal, hopeful, and trusting. Love never fails!"

Finally, he prioritized love as a core value when he stated (v. 13) that "for now there are faith, hope, and love. But of these three, the greatest is love." This is an example of high-level clarity.

We asked a client congregation to identify three to five strongly held values; they chose integrity, freedom, spiritual growth, and honesty. Then we asked them to define each value by asking themselves, *What does this value mean in the life of the congregation?* This is an important step, because most of us assume basic values without questioning them. These congregants were no exception, replying, "Why waste our time? We all know what those words mean." We insisted. Once they began the process of defining their values, they realized that, as with Pastor Jeff and his congregation, they had quite different ideas about what these words actually meant in practice. One member thought that honesty meant being confrontational about what he thought was wrong, while another felt that it didn't include anything that might be perceived as aggression toward other members. It soon became apparent that they had to define values in terms of specific behavior. By doing this, they moved beyond the assumption that "everybody knows" to a practical level, defining their values as behavioral standards for congregational activity. Once they got it, they could move to the next step: prioritizing their values in order of importance to help the congregation determine which areas of ministry to concentrate on first.

Core values precisely reflect who you are. Therefore once you have determined your core values, you must do these four things:

1. Make sure that they are stated clearly.

2. Put them in written form for all to read.

3. Ensure that they are widely known and owned by every member of the congregation.

4. Review and discuss them frequently to keep them before the congregation.

In Part Three, the strategic mapping section of this book, we go into a process of how you can discern your congregation's core values.

Your Mission

Although mission and vision are equal, we have found it practical to concentrate on discovering a congregation's mission as the next step in strategic mapping. Why? Because your mission is your congregation's fundamental reason for being. All ministry activities must be in alignment with it. The mission also takes into account those whom you can serve with quality, and how you serve them. Without this definite commitment to purpose, the visioning process can easily get off track and become little more than a blue-sky exercise.

The Great Commission of the Church

One of Jesus' last acts was to give a specific mission to his followers and to those they would empower: "Go to the people of all nations and make them my disciples. Baptize them in the name of the Father, and the Son, and the Holy Spirit, and teach them to do everything I have told you. I will be with you always, even until the end of the world" (Matthew 28:19–20). There are also four other versions: "Go preach the good news to everyone in the world" (Mark 16:15); "You must tell everything that has happened" (Luke 24:48); "I am sending you, just as the Father has sent me" (John 20:21); and "You will tell everyone about me everywhere in the world" (Acts 1:8). The quote from Matthew, the most complete and concise, is referred to as the Great Commission of the Church. There is disagreement as to whether these are Jesus' actual words, but there is wide acceptance that they are the underpinning of, and the marching orders for, what the Church is called upon to do.

These five citations all add up to one essential point: the disciples were charged with an assignment to preach the good news of the kingdom of God they had heard Jesus preach, the good news that John the Baptizer had preached earlier. The disciples, and those who came after them, did as they were charged. They went to the people of all nations, they preached, they taught, they baptized, and they made disciples, and as they did so the Church grew and prospered. Like the sons of Issachar, the disciples were clear as to their purpose: they "knew the right time to do what needed to be done" (1 Chronicles 12:32).

The Great Commission in the Twenty-First Century

Today, the Church is redefining itself and its concept of how it should carry out its purpose. Let's be clear: its mission has not changed; what is changing are the ways in which the mission is carried out.

As once-prominent mainstream denominations appear to wane, congregations are faced with declining numbers and lack of direction. In *Toward 2015: A Church Odyssey*, Richard Kew and Roger White indicate that by 2015 most congregations with less than 250 members will be unable to do effective ministry—if they exist at all. Moreover, they suggest that if the present downward trend continues, 60 percent of all existing Christian congregations, regardless of current size, will disappear before the year 2050. These breathtaking statements beg the question, "Why is this happening?" Kew and White assert that one of the central reasons is lack of purpose, or mission, in this postmodern era.

If this is the case, why don't congregations do whatever is necessary to clarify their reason for existence? Because, we feel, there are no clear ideas of how best to present the good news in today's world. Part of the challenge lies in our age-old ambiguity about what constitutes the "people of all nations." Mission is still seen as essentially for them and not for us. "They" are conveniently located in far-off places, on the continents of Africa, Asia, and South America, or on some obscure and remote islands in the South Pacific. American and Canadian congregations find it hard to think of "us" as in need of mission.

The Great Commission certainly includes far-off places, but we feel equally certain that it was intended to include us, where we are—right here, right now, in our communities, schools, places of work, and families. Now, as much as they did in earlier times, congregations seek meaning about what God is calling them to do. This requires a clear purpose.

Been There? Done That?

You are probably shaking your head and thinking to yourself, *Here we go again. We've heard it a thousand times. We've already done the work, and we do have a mission statement.* OK, let's make a deal. If you can answer yes without hesitation to these questions, skip this section and head straight for the next part (vision).

- Is your mission statement in total alignment with your stated and defined values?

- Does your mission describe who you are as a community of faith? Does it commit you to transformation? Does it indicate how you will carry this out?

- Are all the actions and activities of your congregational life in alignment with your values and mission?

- Is your mission owned by a majority of your congregation? Can the members state the heart of the mission, if asked?

If you answered no to at least one of these questions, you're not alone. Many congregations have written mission statements but don't have a *mission*. A typical scenario runs like this. The leaders hear that it's important to have a mission statement, so a committee is formed. They spend time thinking about, and crafting, a lengthy, skillfully worded statement. They might have it printed and put on display for a while, and then it ends up collecting dust in a file cabinet. It has become just a piece of paper—a mission statement without a real mission—and the congregation ends up more confused about its identity than it was before they started the process. We've seen this happen many times.

We were called to work with a large and active parish. We got right into the spiritual DNA. The core values exercise went well; they did a good job and were rightly proud of their work. When we turned to mission, however, a team member raised his hand and said, politely but firmly, "You can save us all a lot of time and skip over this section. We've done it." Another team member pointed to the wall behind us and said, "If you'll just look behind you, you'll see our mission." We turned around and caught sight of a beautifully hand-lettered document that had the look of an ancient illumi-nated manuscript. It was double-matted and mounted in a large gilt frame. "See," she continued, "that's been handled." The team's heads all nodded affirmatively in a gotcha attitude.

We congratulated them on a wonderful piece of art and asked the team to turn their chairs a quarter turn so that they faced away from the mission statement. We then asked them a simple question: "Without looking back, would someone please tell us what the mis-sion of this congregation is?" We got a few brave tries, but it was evident to everyone—pastor included—that no one could respond meaningfully. Yes, they had a beautifully framed mission statement, but they did not have a mission. If their mission had been encoded into the life of the congregation, they would have known it and shared it with us easily.

Few congregations understand what mission really is or how to create for themselves a mission statement that is viable and coher-ent. Kew and White comment: "Mission is not a tail to be pinned as an afterthought onto the rear-end of the ecclesiastical donkey. From now on *mission must be the central organizing principle of all the local parish is and all it does.* Once this point has been firmly estab-lished, then it becomes blatantly obvious that all our structures should be geared to enabling mission: if they are not, we must ques-tion whether they have any right to continue existing—and, in the process, devouring increasingly precious resources, time, and tal-ents." (italics in original)

Mission is what motivates and inspires a congregation to do God's work. Marcia Sutton, minister, teacher of clergy, and a respected spiritual director, observes that organizing around a less substantial purpose is like inviting people to a banquet where there is no main course. A congregation with an "appetizer" approach to ministry is likely to believe its growth is tied to structure rather than to substance, to organization and not organism, and to program instead of purpose. The Church does, in fact, offer a magnificent main course: the transformation of individuals, communities, and our world, through a life-changing encounter with the sacred. In "The Rise of Integral Culture," Paul Ray finds that 24 percent of our population—some forty-four million people—whom he calls "cultural creatives" are looking for just that. A mission therefore must offer and celebrate it.

Unfortunately, this has not been communicated clearly by congregations, and many people have turned to secular institutions to fill their needs. Robert Forman, in "Report of Grassroots Spirituality," calls this our "ABC" environment: "anything but the church." Secular institutions do much good and deserve our support, but they do not share the Church's commitment to offer transformation through disciple making. Clarity about the mission of the congregation points the growth effort in the right direction; coupled with core values, this clarity is a starting place for the strategic mapping process.

The Benefits of a Real Mission Statement

"Sell them on the benefits" has been a truism in business for decades. Convincing a congregation about the value of a mission statement has not always been easy, but once people get it, things happen. Look at these sample comments:

> "It's now so clear to us. Our mission spells out who we are and where we're going."

> "Our mission compels us constantly to ask, 'What matters most to us?'"

> "We've discovered the fundamental reason for our existence."

> "For the first time, we have a consistent focus from which to proceed."

Perhaps the ultimate benefit of a well-defined mission is that it gives you direction for being a faithful congregation, just as the rudder of a ship holds the vessel steady through rough times by keeping it on its true course.

A congregation without a well-defined mission lacks purpose. This conversation between Alice and the Cheshire Cat, from Lewis Carroll's *Alice in Wonderland,* says it all:

> "Would you tell me, please, which way I ought to go from here?"
>
> "That depends a good deal on where you want to get to," said the Cat.
>
> "I don't much care where—" said Alice.
>
> "Then it doesn't matter which way you go," said the Cat.
>
> "—so long as I get *somewhere,*" Alice added as an explanation.
>
> "Oh, you're sure to do that," said the Cat, "if only you walk long enough."

Like Alice, many congregations don't seem to know where they are headed, or what they will do once they reach "somewhere," or more important, why they are going there in the first place.

Four Qualities of a Good Mission Statement

A good mission statement has four distinguishing qualities: it's unique, it reflects the congregation's values, the congregants buy into and own it, and they feel accountable to it.

Your Mission Is Unique

A well-stated mission allows seeking people to make comparisons, to see how and why your congregation is different from others in the community, thus helping them decide whether this is the spiritual place for them. Unique, by the way, doesn't necessarily mean that you offer something that no other congregation offers, but rather that you make an effort to inform people of the opportunities for transformation available to them through your congregation.

Your Mission Reflects Your Values

Your mission statement *must* reflect your values, *value by value*. Like an interlocking puzzle, mission and values must agree, so that once in place they allow you to see (envision) the whole picture.

Buy-In and Ownership

An effective congregation starts out with a clear mission. But unless it is constantly clarified in response to change, the mission can quickly be forgotten—or worse, become irrelevant. It's necessary to build a culture of ownership. You can't impose a mission statement from the top down, but you can keep putting the idea out to the congregation until they own it. "Americans are, by nature, rugged individualists, with strong personalities," writes management consultant John Grinnell. "We've got to know 'why' and [then] 'buy-in' to a concept." We've rarely seen anything done well unless people were committed to it. Everyone—especially those in a leadership position in the congregation—needs to buy into the mission statement. Part of their buy-in is the ability to articulate it, if not word for word then at least its essence.

Accountability to the Mission

With buy-in and ownership comes accountability. To what or whom are people and teams accountable? How can accountability be measured? The first step in accountability is to be clear about boundaries. Of course, your spiritual DNA sets up the ultimate boundaries. As Anthony De Mello said, like a river, spiritual DNA creates its own banks and its own natural flow. Let your potential leaders know, *before* they accept a position of leadership, that your ministry activities are not disjointed stand-alones, that there are no Lone Rangers in your congregation, that everyone is accountable.

A good beginning is to create a written job description stating the purpose and function of every ministry activity, a description that contains a statement of how the activity, and the leaders of that activity, support (are accountable to) your mission. It gives the congregation a tool by which it can measure whether the activity is doing what it is designed to do. If not fulfilling its promise, the activity should be discontinued. Let's be clear on what we mean by job description. We're not suggesting that you get overly bureaucratic and create a maze of unnecessary paperwork. A job description in our context is a brief, succinctly written, permission-giving outline of a particular task.

Accountability isn't intended as a restrictive management technique that's imposed on a congregation. Accountability was clearly part of Jesus' ministry. He taught his followers, trained them, and reflected (followed up) with them. He sent them out on practice missions to give them experience in preaching and dealing with people, and they returned to Jesus, "and told him everything they had done and taught" (Mark 6:30). At first, he set boundaries by limiting where they should evangelize. Later, in the Great Commission, those boundaries were expanded to include the whole world. Paul was equally clear that accountability was important, especially regarding behavior. He fully expected people not only to be able to talk the talk but to walk the walk, as demonstrated in their own personal lives.

Being accountable means that individuals are responsible for their actions. It means doing the best one can in any given situation. It means being responsible to the great trust that has been extended to the individual by the congregation. Accountability is an understanding by each individual, each group, each team, that all congregational activities are connected to a common mission, and that people and activities are working for the good of the whole.

Make It a Thoughtful Process

We North Americans are an impatient people. "Get that done by yesterday," we hear, which causes us to act in haste and often results in wasted effort and time.

Some parish leaders shared with us how they discovered that. They had spent a long day working on particularly thorny problems. Just before adjournment, someone reminded them of one final item on the agenda: a mission statement. They each grabbed a sheet of paper and scribbled down some comments. They were too tired to be particularly creative, so they used standard "mission-type" words and phrases that didn't signify much but sounded good. Then they cobbled their efforts together into a few sentences. Someone pointed out that they had forgotten to include God, so they threw the word in for good measure, tweaked it some more, read it aloud, and pronounced it finished—all within thirty minutes. But did they have a real mission? Apparently not. When they later called us in to rescue them, they were despondent over their lack of common purpose.

Having spent the last decade reading mission statements, we can say with some authority that many missions are neither clear nor simply stated. A client congregation included the word *covenant* in its mission statement. It's a fine and appropriate word, but when we asked them what it meant, in the context of the life and work of the congregation, they couldn't tell us. After some probing, it turned out they'd heard it was the latest denominational buzzword and included it because it was trendy!

Say what you mean, and say it in standard language. It isn't necessary for people to ooh and ahh over the beauty of the language, but they must be able to understand it.

Benjamin Franklin once wrote to a friend, "I'm sorry that I didn't have time to write you a short letter." Powerful statements do not need to be long, nor do they need flowery language. Your mission statement should be concise, creative, descriptive, believable, understandable, motivating, achievable—and *short*. But keep Franklin's point in mind: brevity takes time.

The mission statement of Riverbend Church in Austin, Texas, is an excellent example: "Our mission is to reach out to the bruised, battered, broken, and bored of this world with a message of acceptance and grace from the God who loves them."

This congregation is not only united in its purpose—to reach out—but also clear about the target market. "The bruised, battered, broken, and bored" speaks eloquently to the image of the congregation as a place for souls yearning for transformation.

What is their offer of transformation? It's a message of love and acceptance. It's an offer that can be understood and appreciated by contemporary people who quickly get a sense of what River-bend Church is about.

Key Components of a Mission Statement

Every mission statement has three key components:

1. It defines identity (*who* you are).
2. It identifies transformation as the primary task (*what* you do) and often includes for whom.
3. It indicates *how* you will carry this out.

Let's look at these in relation to the Great Commission:

1. Define identity. The Church has a universality that encompasses everyone ("Go to the people of all nations . . .").
2. Primary task. The primary task of the Church is discipleship—through the transforming love of God (". . . and make them my disciples . . .").
3. Carry through. How will this be carried out? Through bringing people into the life and work of the congregation ("Baptize them . . . and teach them all that I have taught you").

Note the concise language. The Great Commission is a condensed strategy for building the kingdom of God, and it clearly summarizes who, what, and how.

The mission statement of First United Methodist Church of Salem, Oregon, is: "We are a diverse and inclusive community of faith, seeking to follow the example of Jesus Christ by *welcoming* all to a walk with Christ, *nurturing* each other in Christian love, *equipping* people with a faith that works in real life, and *serving* God in the church, the community and the world."

By scanning their mission, we can see how they met the three-part criteria:

1. Define identity. How does First Church describe itself? As "a diverse and inclusive community of faith. . . ."
2. Primary task. How will transformation be effected? By "following the example of Jesus Christ. . . ."
3. Carry through. How will they do this? By "*welcoming* all to a walk with Christ, *nurturing* each other in Christian love, *equipping* people with a faith that works in real life, and *serving* God in the church, the community and the world."

This mission statement is clear and concise, and it tells us *how* First Church intends to build the kingdom of God.

We'll cover the how-to process of creating your mission statement as part of strategic mapping in Chapter Seven.

Your Vision of Your Future

Michelangelo's monumental *David* is an example of vision made palpable. Long before Michelangelo ever picked up his chisel and began carving, he had a vision: his thoughts, impressions, and ideas of what the rough marble block before him could become. We don't know how many forms of David were caught inside that marble block, or what form some other sculptor might have released from the same stone. We do know that the *David* that did emerge was born of Michelangelo's vision: a composite of all his thoughts, feelings, impressions, and ideas.

Seek God's Vision

Vision and mission are often used interchangeably, but they are distinct in an important way. Your mission and your core values are precise statements. Vision, on the other hand, is simple and evocative, and this simplicity can have a profound influence on the behavior of the congregation.

As you work to discern your vision, keep in mind that it is God's vision for you that you seek. "I reveal myself to them in visions, I speak to them in dreams" (Numbers 12:6, NIV). We believe that God speaks to us, and that we each perceive God's voice in different ways. Some hear it as an interior voice speaking to them; others feel it in persistent hunches, and gentle nudges. What you are looking for is what God has in mind for your congregation. True vision comes from beyond you and is always larger than life, yet is within you and is part of your congregational life. You must be captured by a vision of God's greatness, or you can never have a full and complete picture of your work. To paraphrase Proverbs 29:18, where there is no vision, ministry perishes. Without a vision, you and your congregation can find yourselves going nowhere fast.

Vision causes you to answer these questions: "Are we doing this for our own glory?" "Are we missing something God is trying to tell us?" "Are we in danger of becoming proud and forgetting that whatever we are, or have accomplished, is through God's grace?" Vision begins with your spirituality, *not* with your work; it is from this spiritual encounter with God that you see the possibilities to which God is calling you. Perhaps, like Isaiah (6:8), you will respond, "I'll go. Send me!"

What Is a Vision?

Like your mission, your vision reflects your core values. But unlike your mission, your vision can change and be replaced by a new desired state. A vision is a desired future reality, a hoped for result, that captures the heart and mind in such a compelling way that people are willing to commit their resources of time, talent, and treasure to make it a reality. A congregation's vision consists of those thoughts, ideas, and feelings that it really cherishes and brings into reality. It is a powerful mental image of what you want to create. It reflects what you care about most by focusing on what you want to accomplish within the boundaries set by your values and your mission. It is an ever-evolving mosaic of pictures that are the result of successfully implementing your mission.

In fact, all vision statements need further expansion, particularly as a congregation moves in the direction of the dream. As your vision evolves over time, you will want to revisit it periodically to ensure that it adequately reflects your direction; of course, it can be updated as necessary. A vision is about the community's well-being, now and into the future. It answers the question, What will success look like? It is the pursuit of this image that motivates people to work together. Stephen S. Wise summed it up beautifully in these words: "Vision looks inward and becomes duty. Vision looks outward and becomes aspiration. Vision looks upward and becomes faith."

We can also say that a vision paints a picture of the future. We've seen that Jesus painted word pictures of his vision of the kingdom of God. Two other familiar visions are those of the prophet Isaiah (11:6–9) and Martin Luther King Jr. Both used rich imagery and everyday examples as they painted word pictures so real one can easily visualize them. Isaiah's picture was of a world of peace and harmony; he used traditional images of antagonists who would one day live side by side. King communicated his vision on the steps of the Lincoln Memorial in Washington, D.C. "I have a dream," he said, and he too used rich imagery as he described a time when all people, regardless of race, would be equal. He painted a vision so compelling that America changed as a nation.

Similarly, a congregation uses images and metaphors to paint pictures that are intended to stimulate the imagination and draw the mind into a place filled with expectation, excitement, and wonder. Yet vision is more. It is a process that includes evaluating present conditions, identifying problem areas, and bringing about a general agreement on how to overcome problems and manage change for a better future. The truth is that so long as the congregation is healthy and alive, new paintings that reflect an overarching vision will be produced. Thereafter, specificity is introduced into these pictures of a desired future through goals and objectives.

How a Vision Can Become Reality

Let's look at how the vision process worked at Living Enrichment Center (LEC) in Wilsonville, Oregon, a church founded by senior minister Mary Manin Morrissey in 1974. We've worked with Mary and this congregation, and we tell this story in some detail to portray how a vision can progress from the dream stage to an actual envisioned reality. This is a story of inspiration and faith; above all, it's a story of keeping focused on the future. Jonathan Swift wrote, "Vision is the art of seeing things invisible."

For the first ten years, fifty was a good Sunday attendance for LEC. On some Sundays, Mary and her husband were the only members of the congregation. But as they began clarifying their purpose, attendance started to climb, and they moved from location to location to accommodate the growing congregation. By 1984, attendance was more than one hundred. Then it moved up to five hundred, and way up to twelve hundred. At that level, it was clear that they needed a permanent site, and planning began. Then Mary heard God say to her, "Don't build the building now; build people now." Finding a new location wasn't as important as knowing how God would unfold their next step, so after Easter 1991 they began a visioning process. They started with the transformational core of their mission: "healing lives and building dreams." How could they carry it out? What would this look like? They needed a format, so they used a storyboarding process.

They wrote the current year (1991) at one end of the storyboard and 1994 at the opposite end. This became their frame of reference as they began envisioning "pictures" of how they wanted their church to look and what they wanted it to be. All pictures were to be in the first person, so to speak, as though they were a reality now, following the promise of Jesus in Mark 11:24: "Everything you ask for in prayer will be yours, if you only have faith."

It was exciting as people's pictures came into focus: "I see people coming from all over to attend services." "I see a wonderful sanctuary surrounded by acres of trees." "I see us working together in fun and fellowship." "I see a wonderful space for the children, and there's an outdoor play area, too." Others saw "spacious parking," "luscious, landscaped gardens," and "a large statue of Jesus with outstretched arms." The children were included in the process, and from their vision perspective they saw a swimming pool in their ideal church. That gave people pause; a swimming pool?

They next turned their attention to that wide-open space on the storyboard between the two dates of Easter 1991 and Easter 1994. How would they get from where they were now to where they wanted to be in the future? Using four-by-six index cards, they named and listed every possible obstacle they could think of: finding land, hiring an architect, creating plans, raising money, getting permits, choosing furniture and carpeting. Later on, they would work on the specifics of these challenges, but for the purpose of this process they arranged their cards in order of accomplishment on the time line and created a storyboard for their dream. It was kept on display so the congregation could keep the dream before their eyes.

Did they know how they were going to reach their goal? Not at all. They had no land and little money. "What we did have," Mary says, "was our knowledge that the mind is a tool of vision, so we created a collective vision in our minds. Paul wrote, 'We live by faith, not by what we see.' Faith means stepping out and taking one step at a time."

In October 1991, the members of the congregation were asked to write vision statements for their spiritual home. All the statements were collected and read publicly. Among them:

> We have a beautiful spiritual home, a campus with landscaping that reflects God's beauty, trees, flowers . . . meditation gardens with benches and resting places, and statues of holy people. . . .
>
> Our spiritual home is large enough to serve our congregation with room for expansion. . . .

The sanctuary is a simple and yet elegant place in which to worship. . . .

We enjoy natural light streaming in to bless all in attendance. . . .

As the church's children are of high priority, we invest in lavish youth facilities and children's play areas. . . .

We have surplus parking for all the people who attend services, classes, support groups, and seminars. . . .

We have a kitchen large enough to meet the fellowship and special event needs of this dynamic congregation. . . .

The facilities are ecologically sound and environmentally pleasing.

The written statements were then crafted into a cohesive vision. Now that they had given specificity to their dream, they focused, in faith, and with only $100,000 in the building fund—not enough even for a down payment on a piece of property—they stepped out in faith and the search began. The power of vision is compelling; people came forward, new ideas were presented, and a site was located. It was a large rehabilitation center, located in Wilsonville, a suburb of Portland, built by the state at a cost of $8 million and up for sale. The congregation was able to work the asking price down from $4 million to $3 million, but they still needed $1 million to be able to move in. In just four months, two thousand visionary people pledged the $1 million, and the miracle happened: the congregation was able to move into its own home.

Did the specifics of their vision become a reality? You decide for yourself. The ninety-five-acre campus is surrounded by tall trees. There are nature trails winding through the trees. A large bronze statue of Jesus with outstretched arms, modeled after the Christ of the Andes, welcomes all people. The 97,000-square-foot building, large enough to serve four thousand people, houses a seven-hundred-seat sanctuary. There are lots of classrooms, play areas, a spacious bookstore, and a large industrial kitchen. Remember the kids' far-fetched vision? On site, there is an indoor swimming pool that's nearly Olympic size! The Sunday Children's Celebration attracts 250 kids. The campus has a retreat center available to church and civic groups, with cabins for overnight stays. There are beautifully land-scaped gardens, there's a pond, a youth building, and plenty of park-ing. In keeping with their vision, the facilities are ecologically and environmentally sound. From a handful of people in the pastor's liv-ing room, they have become a "full-service" congregation operating seven days a week and ministering to thousands.

Happily, as we have just seen, a vision assists in seeing beyond today by producing a clear view of a new reality a congregation can create, and a process of how the reality will unfold. The paradox is that though vision draws us toward the future, its unfolding is expe-rienced in the present.

So what is your dream, your vision, your picture of the future?

The Pastor as Vision Caster and Vision Bearer

The values, mission, and vision of the congregation must be consis-tently lifted up by the chief vision caster, the individual most respon-sible for articulating the spiritual DNA of the congregation: the pastor. As a vision caster, the pastor constantly reminds the congregants of who they are, what they believe in, and what God is calling them to become. The pastor is also a vision bearer, one who models the values that will make the vision—the dream of the future—a reality, and who creates unity of purpose by articulating them over and over in mes-sages and sermons, and by painting the picture of the desired future.

For a pastor, vision casting has the potential to be a powerful aspect of communication. The great preacher Henry Ward Beecher once said, "The ability to convert visions to things is the secret of success." Vision expands the ability to see and acknowledge what is going on around you and in you. If the vision is to take hold and make a difference in your congregation's ministry, and ultimately in the lives of people, it must be heard, understood, and embraced by as many as possible. The importance of communicating cannot be overemphasized. Without buy-in and help from all relevant parties, chances of successful vision casting are slim. This is why the pastor's role is so important.

It's Tough to Cast a Vision When . . .

We often meet dispirited pastors who feel that they've somehow done something wrong because not many people are involved in the work of ministry, or because more haven't caught the vision of what the congregation can truly become. It's tough being a vision caster when the pastor ends up with responsibility for most aspects of ministry—from making all the pastoral calls to getting to the church early and brewing coffee for Sunday fellowship; from being responsible for greeting all the newcomers to being sensitive to the nurturing needs of existing congregants; from teaching the Bible class to vacuuming the carpet. Is this what vision casting is about, they ask?

Our advice to those pastors is not to be too hard on themselves. It's taken congregations decades to solidify the hierarchical top-down model where the pastor alone engages in ministry while congregants are largely passive. It's not possible, in a matter of a few months (or perhaps even years), to completely reverse this process. What can be done, however, is to make sure that the pastor and key lay-leaders have done some basic work of clarifying the congregation's spiritual identity—its DNA. Once this is done, the pastor is the primary vision caster who lifts up the dream of renewal and growth.

Success will come, but it's one day at a time. Remember, the congregation got to where it is one step at a time. It will move into the future the same way, one step at a time. Some prefer to stay put, stay secure. This is the time for pastor and leaders to begin listening when people say, "We can't do that," and work to transform and heal those can't-do-its to can-do-its. The pastor's crucial role, then, is to lift up the dream of a renewed future, even when congregants can't see where the future may take them.

As vision caster and vision bearer, there is no more effective rule a pastor can remember than that suggested by the German poet Goethe: "Whatever you can do, or dream you can, begin it. Boldness has genius, power, and magic in it." Why not begin it now?

Part II

Using "WelNES" Systems to Renew and Grow Your Congregation

If one part of our body hurts, we hurt all over. If one part of our body is honored, the whole body will be happy.

1 Corinthians 12:26

In Part One, we identified the three essential components of your congregation's spiritual DNA: core values, mission, and vision. To be effective, these must enliven all parts of the organism. This is the job of *systems*. Just as the circulatory system makes sure blood carries nutrients to every part of the human body, congregational systems help maintain overall health in the body of Christ. This healthy growth expresses itself not only in adding more members to the congregation but in the deepening, rooting, and renewing of individuals and (through this growth) renewing of the congregation.

The body of Christ incorporates a great many systems that affect the organic development of the congregation. Four key systems, however, have the greatest impact on the life of a healthy congregation. We use the acronym WelNES, derived from the four systems: welcoming, nurturing, empowering, and serving.

These systems are intended to deliver the congregation's spiritual DNA throughout the body effectively and consistently. To determine if this is happening, you assess the current state of the system through the evaluative tools found in Chapter Seven. Once you've determined the level of health, you choose tactics that best reflect your identity and competence, and then you commit to carrying them out with quality over a set period of time, say six months. You use this time interval to monitor the effects of the systemic changes you've made. If the tactic produces a stronger, more vital system, keep it. If it does not produce the kind of results you intend, replace it with another and track the new tactic's efficacy.

We explore these key systems separately in the next four chapters. Please keep in mind, however, that these systems are *not* independent; they are *inter*dependent. They are constantly interacting with one another to maintain the health of the organism.

Moreover, these systems are present, as we've noted, to deliver wellness. But you may also think of this process as one of facilitating wholeness, which in our understanding is what transformation is about.

When Jesus urged the early Church to go out into the world and make disciples, we believe he was talking about people experiencing transformation not just as a one-time encounter but as an ongoing process. It's a process beginning with a welcoming system that builds friendships; it then continues with a nurturing system that creates discipleship, deepens with an empowering system that introduces stewardship, and expands through a serving system that creates opportunity for servant-leadership. Through a systemic approach to strengthening friendship, discipleship, stewardship, and leadership, your congregation can become the healthy organism God intends it to be.

3

Come Right In

Your Welcoming System

Driving on U.S. I-90 West across South Dakota is rather uneventful until one encounters the desolate beauty of the Black Hills and the Badlands. Even reading billboards becomes rote after a while . . . until you see those ever-present signs for Wall Drug ("just 250 miles ahead"). There are so many of them along the highway, you begin to wonder if Wall Drug actually exists. Finally, you pull into the little town of Wall, population 800, the home indeed of Wall Drug: a unique place with store after store of tourist items, everything from moccasins to rattlesnake eggs, and a cafe that seats 520. Thousands of tourists make their way there annually, almost as if on a pilgrimage. The story of Wall Drug may seem an odd inclusion in a book aimed at congregations, but it is a fine illustration of a welcoming system that works.

In 1931, Ted and Dorothy Hustead moved from Nebraska to Wall (whose population was then 326) to open a drug store. Wall Drug started small, and for the first five years it remained small— too small for the Husteads. They wrestled with the problem of attracting people to their place of business; without steady customers, they'd always be a small store in a small town. Then, during the summer of 1936, Dorothy came up with a brilliant idea. A scorching heat wave was sweeping across the Badlands, and everyone was hot and tired (these were the days before air conditioning). Dorothy reasoned that travelers driving through the area would be pretty uncomfortable, so she convinced Ted to post signs along the highway advertising "free ice water ahead." This act of hospitality, of welcoming the stranger, drew people to Wall Drug. More than sixty years later, they are still coming in the thousands.

Welcoming people to a community of faith, of course, requires more than a series of catchy signs. Welcoming is a spiritual concept so basic that the Jewish, Christian, and Islamic traditions use the same illustration. For Christians and Jews, it's found in Genesis 18.

Genesis 18 tells the story of the venerable patriarch Abraham and his wife, Sarah, who, having lived long lives, did not have the son and heir they longed and prayed for. The old couple had pitched their tent under the shade of the great oak trees at Mamre. One day, Abraham saw three strangers coming across the desert; according to custom he rushed to greet them and offered water, bread, and shade under the oaks. Sarah cooked for the strangers and waited upon their every need.

It's a great story of people being nice to people they don't know. But there is more. It's also about the benefits that can accrue from being hospitable to newcomers, for the three strangers were messengers sent from God who announced to Sarah that even in her advanced age she would bear a son, Isaac, who would be the progenitor of the people of Israel. Had Abraham and Sarah turned their backs on these messengers and refused them hospitality, they would not have received God's wonderful news.

Newcomers first experience you through your welcoming system. But how do you experience them? As intruders, or as messengers from God? Being a welcoming congregation means receiving individuals into your presence warmly and lovingly, as though they were sent from God. True welcoming calls us to move beyond our own needs, tensions, and worries and begin to see our visitors not simply as guests but, in the words of Henri Nouwen, as "Christ incognito."

Your welcoming system is a living, interconnected, interrelated way to deliver the spiritual DNA throughout the body of Christ—your congregation. It is organized around a specific function: to attract and welcome newcomers. Welcoming really has five parts:

1. Understanding that welcoming is more than a handshake and a smile; it requires spiritual preparation

2. Attracting newcomers to your spiritual community

3. Knowing something about who the newcomers are and what they are seeking

4. Exploring visitor-friendly welcoming

5. Establishing follow-up methods for the newcomer's visits

A Theology of Hospitality

Welcoming is not about "noses and nickels," that is, filling your pews so you can pay your bills. Welcoming only for such a reason creates a pathology that is harmful to newcomers and to the congregation. You implement a strong welcoming system not because you need to but because it's the right thing to do; it represents who you are.

To be authentic, the act of attracting and welcoming must reflect your congregation's DNA. Reaching out requires understanding, and perhaps rethinking, the role of your congregation. It means understanding that the local church is not your property; it belongs to God. The members of your congregation are stewards and custodians of it for God. You welcome people to God's house, to a safe place where God receives them as they are and heals them. You welcome them to a place of renewal, to a place where they can build lasting relationships with God and others. The purpose of the congregation, first and foremost, is to carry out God's work by making opportunities for transforming individuals and the community.

Reaching out—welcoming—is more than a friendly smile and a handshake at the entrance of the church, important as those gestures are. True welcoming is the natural result of a heartfelt belief that you have something important and precious to offer. It is based on your understanding that people have a deep-seated spiritual need for a connection with the sacred. It is the belief that your congregation is a place where people can make these connections with their true selves and with others. Reaching out is prompted by a sincere and compelling desire to share the good news as you have received it. A congregation welcomes people not because they hope to benefit from it (though they often do), and not because it's nice to be nice, which it is. It is not an act of altruism. Welcoming is central to our spiritual traditions.

The welcoming system is potentially transformative for those being welcomed *and* for those extending the welcome. The newcomer is able to see, as Nouwen said, the face of Christ in the smile of the hosts or in the cheery greeting of the person next to them in the pew, or in the warmth of the people who greet others during the fellowship time after the service. The person carrying out the welcoming grows spiritually by helping to carry out the mission of the congregation. The congregation as a whole benefits from an expanded life in God. That's the beauty of the welcoming system: it works for all who participate in it.

We're Friendly—But to Whom?

We haven't met a congregation yet that doesn't shout from the steeple top just how friendly it is, even though few people return and visitors tell their friends that they neither felt welcome nor found the congregation particularly friendly.

A parish we worked with has a massive complex of buildings reflecting an era when thousands were attracted to the congregation. When we were there, about forty showed up on a good Sunday to worship in a sanctuary designed for seven hundred. Many of these folks still sit where they have sat for years—forty people scattered around a seven-hundred-seat auditorium.

Even more fascinating is how they access the sanctuary. The church has a beautiful circular driveway, but it is more convenient to park in the rear lot and use the ramp that connects with the gymnasium door. Then it's a matter of a simple walk through several rooms and across the foyer to the sanctuary. Over time, things reached the point of neglecting even to unlock and open the great carved front doors. The rationale was obvious: we enter through the back, so there's no need to open them. Of course, this meant they'd have no Sunday visitors. Here was a welcoming system in need of emergency care.

Our first recommendation was pretty simple: open the front doors! People protested. The wind would blow in. Heating costs would rise. But they did agree, finally, to open just one of the three doors. Now that a door was open, we took them on a journey of self-discovery to see whom they might welcome inside.

Their neighborhood had changed—racially, economically, and culturally. The congregation had to decide whether it was within their spiritual DNA to open up to newcomers who did not look like them but whose needs were just as important. Thankfully, they decided that inclusion—one of their core values—was more than a word and could only be expressed in new forms of ministry. They began to look at the needs of their surrounding area, and how they might be met. Working with community leaders, they planned and funded a multicultural center for the arts, using their facilities for education, training, and public performances. They opened their doors—and opened their hearts as well.

Another congregation asked us to evaluate their Sunday welcoming process. We entered the beautiful "carpenter gothic" building a few minutes before service time. A small assemblage was present. We had just settled into an empty pew near the back of the church when two members came up behind us and began talking in a stage whisper that could be heard across town: "Should we tell them they're sitting in our pew?" From this comment, and from several other uninviting things they did, it was clear that the congregation thought of the church as their space, not as God's space with God's pews waiting to seat God's people, whether they are regulars or not.

Situations of this kind are not unusual. They often happen in an existing congregation, where "antibodies" fight successful infusion of newcomers. Even after a decade of consulting, we're amazed at the typical response in answer to the question, "Are you a welcoming and friendly congregation?" The initial reply is, "Of course, we are." After some probing, the discussion almost always reveals that they are friendly to each other, but not necessarily to newcomers. If, in fact, they were open and welcoming to those seeking a faith community, the welcoming system would produce positive results.

Another comment masks a core of hostility toward the newcomer: "Well, it takes two for this to work, you know. They have to meet us halfway." This, however, is a flawed view. Any congregation that presents itself as a "public temple" has a responsibility to share God's love with all who enter. Those who have grown from this relationship with God and know its benefits must enthusiastically reach out to those making their first tentative exploration of the Church.

We occasionally hear, "There aren't that many who would be interested." In fact, George Barna reports that two-thirds of unchurched people say that being asked to church would have a positive effect on them. That's the rub—*if they were asked*. Most congregations with few visitors seldom make the effort to invite people. It's almost as if they know they don't have their act together and don't want to be embarrassed by having a stranger discover the truth. Those congregations are really not ready to handle newcomers. "Although it is not a popular notion," Barna writes, "sometimes churches fail to attract the unchurched because God is protecting both the church and the unchurched from each other."

The welcoming system, then, is integral to the Great Commission. You cannot make disciples of those whom you are not willing to welcome. You cannot extend hospitality to those about whom you are not concerned. You cannot truly welcome people if you are not ready to hear their stories and to accept them, wherever they may be on their journey of faith. Each time you welcome others, you grow, even if the newcomer never returns.

Who Is Coming to Church?

Whether they are actively seeking a church home or just passing through, you want guests to feel welcome, and to know something about you. To do this with excellence requires basic knowledge of your potential guests.

A typical newcomer lives within your ministry area and has not been involved in the life of a congregation for at least six months. Many are seeking to fulfill one or more of three main goals:

1. They are seeking a spiritual basis and a meaning for life that materialism has not been able to provide.

2. They feel a strong need to belong, to be part of something greater than themselves, to establish meaningful relationships with God and with others in community.

3. An increasing number of newcomers with young children say they are looking for ways to strengthen the family structure; they want to learn skills relating to good parenting, and they want their children to learn positive life values.

What Brings Them Here?

Families may choose your congregation because of the excellence of your children's ministry. Others come for ethnic or cultural considerations. Some may come for linguistic homogeneity. A preponderance of a particular lifestyle segment, such as singles or young marrieds, will attract others. The proximity of your congregation to people's homes attracts them. Or they may share your congregation's appreciation of diversity, and your openness to alternative lifestyles. There are also the "church shoppers," looking for a community of faith; and the "church hoppers," who are jumping from one congregation to another in search of the "right" church home. People are drawn to congregations for many reasons, but primarily for spirituality and community.

Relationship to the Church

People's relationships to the Church cover a vast spectrum of experience. Newcomers may have little or no church background, or they may have sudden need for spiritual guidance, or they may be people who are returning after many years.

Little or No Church Background

The first group of folks have little or no memory or experience of congregational life. They are looking for a place where their spiritual needs can be met. Researchers have estimated that 60 percent of Generation-Xers have little or no connection with church life. Two stories are illustrative.

Becky Daniel's young adult son, David, is unchurched. He and his wife have a two-month-old baby, and he called his mother to inform her that they were planning a "baptismal party." Their friends had just had one for their child. It was fun, and they thought it would be great for their baby. She asked a question that's natural to churched folks: "Oh, David, that's wonderful; when is the baby being baptized?" Stunned silence on the other end of the phone, and then, "Baptized? Mom, what's that got to do with the party?"

Kevin Michaelson, a young person new to the Church, related how he was baptized. His mother had never been to a church in her life, but she had heard that children ought to be baptized. She was not clear as to the concept, but she understood the methodology, so one morning she put her baby son in the kitchen sink and ran the water over him to baptize him!

Both of these stories underscore how disconnected the role of faith can be from an important life transition.

Traumatic Experience

One of the most powerful reasons people give for seeking out the Church is that they have had a traumatic experience—divorce, death, loss of a relationship, family breakdown, work difficulty, even the loss of a pet—in the past few months. These newcomers are often hurting souls seeking guidance and direction from a faith community.

A pastor called on us to evaluate her congregation's new "contemporary" service. It was informal, with lots of interaction, and at one point she asked if anyone would like to share what brought them to the service. A few stood and made some pleasant comments. Finally, a man began his story by saying that he had not been involved in church life for about twelve years, though he lived a few blocks away. He and his wife were having marital difficulties, he suspected her of seeing someone else, and the whole situation went progressively from bad to worse. Two nights ago, he came home and found his house empty, his family gone, and their joint bank account cleaned out. A note was taped on a kitchen cabinet, stating tersely that his wife had left and taken their kids and most of the possessions with her. He was devastated, and he burst into tears. "I don't know what to do," he said, "I'm so lonely." He came to the congregation almost as a last resort, but it turned out to be his best move. He came to a caring place that was willing to take him as he was; through prayer and counseling, they helped him get back on his feet.

Nominally Churched

Newcomers, with some memory of congregational life, are sometimes referred to as the nominally churched. Approximately 65 percent of Baby Boomers dropped out of church life in their younger years. They have not found their answers through secular means and want to give the Church a second try. Others return so their children can be exposed to a community of faith. Some, unfortunately, find that there has been little change and the situations that caused them to leave in the first place are still operable.

People Who Respond to Your Ministry

Others conversant with church culture, teachings, and language occasionally "transfer" from one congregation to another. One common reason is geographical relocation; the church is in their neighborhood. Another reason is that they respond to some special aspect of ministry.

Gil and Sue were active Roman Catholics. They enrolled their daughter, Megan, in the children's program of their church, but she became bored with it and tried everything possible not to attend. Then a neighbor introduced them to a kids' program at a local Presbyterian church. It was packed with young children who appeared to love to go to Sunday school. Gil and Sue let Megan attend a few sessions. She came home enthusiastic about the place, and wanted to continue. Though the parents thought of themselves as good Catholics, in the interest of their daughter they began attending the Presbyterian church. When asked about the potential faith conflict, they said their child's spiritual education was paramount. "Maybe, someday," Sue said, "when Megan's grown up, we'll go back to being Catholics."

Five Generations in the Church

There are 128 generational references in the Hebrew scriptures and 163 in the Christian scriptures, so it's not a novel idea to look at the spiritual needs of people according to age. There are now five distinct generations in the Church, each with its own needs.

GI Generation

This generation (people born between 1900 and 1929) was challenged by the Great Depression and tested by World War II. In both instances, they responded with creativity and determination. TV news anchor Tom Brokaw called them "America's greatest generation." At the end of World War II, because of the GI Bill, they entered universities in record numbers; they also married in record numbers and produced children in the millions. This phenomenon affected all of this nation's institutions, including the Church. Large facilities were built to meet the expanding numbers for worship and children's programs. This take-charge generation basically set the pattern for worship and programs still in effect in many congregations.

Silent Generation

The Silent Generation (born between 1930 and 1945) was raised during the Depression, too young for World War II, and too old for the Vietnam conflict. The Silents—a stable and adaptive generation— did all they could to continue and secure congregational growth initiated by their predecessors. Silents prefer formal liturgy and an intellectual approach to programming. Silents can expect to live longer than any previous generation, so there is a definite market for church events that focus on health and wellness, finance, self-fulfillment, and service opportunities. Some Silents are part of the sandwich phenomenon: they are caring for aging parents and also for their own adult children, who, having a hard time making ends meet, have returned home.

There are now more Americans over age sixty-five than there are under eighteen. The number of people over sixty is growing three times faster than the population at large. The GI and Silent Generations have time to give to a congregation, a high level of institutional commitment, and an enormous reservoir of maturity and wisdom to share with other generations. In addressing the needs of these folks, a congregation should be age-sensitive.

Baby Boom Generation

The Baby Boomers (born between 1946 and 1964) are the most heavily researched cohort thanks to their sheer numbers (more than seventy-six million) and their energy. More than any other generation, Baby Boomers have changed the face of the North American Church. Comfortable with praise music, technology, and marketing strategies, this generation has created most of the huge megachurches (five thousand or more members) to serve the needs of unchurched seekers. Boomers are now in control of many institutions in society and in the Church, and they have inherited the problems created when their fellow Boomers left in the 1960s.

Boomers must now take on responsibilities in relation to their own aging, those of their aging parents, and their GenX and Millennial children. This is a massive undertaking, but Boomers have proved time and again that they are capable of facilitating great change. Many, spurred by the desire to give their children some religious education, have returned to the Church, though with a level of skepticism. This is not surprising. This generation of analyzers compares and contrasts; they weigh the "cost" of engaging with a congregation against the potential benefits. If they perceive the engagement as a negative, they exit just as quickly as they returned.

Generation X

Born between 1965 and 1983, Gen-Xers, like the Silents, are largely adaptive. Their life-views and daily struggles are portrayed in the popular TV series "Friends." They are the grown-up latchkey kids; they have experienced the devastation of AIDS, and its implications have shaped their perspectives. Though instant wealth may be possible for a few in dot com companies, this is the poorest of the adult generations. They suffer from being in the shadow of the Boomers and resent being thought of as young Boomers. Many if not most of this generation have little memory of the Church. They are a tough sell for most mainstream congregations.

Millennial Generation

Reaching the Millennials (born after 1984) is even more difficult. Projections are that this generation will exceed the Boomers in size and be the largest generation in American history. Millennials were born into a burgeoning technological age, with all its advances and advantages. They take personal computers, cell phones, and credit cards for granted. They appear to have more fascination with mysticism and developing the interior life than previous generations. Moreover, they do not perceive a conflict between science and religion, and are open to exploring a new postliterate experiential Christianity through drama, visual arts, liturgy, and dance.

Reaching Gen-Xers and Millennials

Given these daunting descriptions, how can you foster an environment in which spiritual growth is possible? In our experience, the congregation that is best able to meet the needs of postmoderns—Gen-Xers and Millennials—is the one that stresses relationships to be explored and strengthened in community. Participation is a given in this type of spiritual community. People come to know each other, grow with each other, and provide support and encouragement for one another. It will be a 24/7 community, available twenty-four hours a day, seven days a week. It is a community interested in mystical spirituality, yet one that would process that spirituality through contemporary music as well as Gregorian chant, through incense and through video, through the organ and through CDs. This postmodern period is a time of paradox in which anything goes. It is also a time of incredible opportunity for a congregation choosing to meet the challenges.

The Multigenerational Myth

Most congregations, in their heart of hearts, want to be multigenerational and serve the needs of all groups. It's a noble dream, but it's not always realistic. No congregation can meet the needs of all groups with quality; it simply does not have the resources (money, people, space, expertise). There is often serious conflict around this issue, particularly in a congregation with an older constituency. The congregants genuinely want to reach out to other generations, and they genuinely do not want to change those fundamental aspects of their identity, such as music and liturgy, which they cherish. They are saying, in effect, "We want to be multigenerational—as long as we stay in control and continue doing things exactly as we've always done."

One congregation we observed lost an entire generation by enticing them to join but refusing to give them a role in the affairs of the parish. This congregation now has a very small Millennial population, and a preponderant group of seniors. They have no middle generations. Their future will be interesting to watch. Unless there is a commitment to share decision making among the age cohorts, there can be little hope of developing multigenerational ministry. There are encouraging signs, however, as congregations become aware of the problem and work to design creative solutions.

The bottom line is this: it's going to get more and more difficult to involve younger people in the Church unless congregations are willing to embrace change as an opportunity for growth rather than as a threat. To know how to respond requires, first and foremost, carefully listening to each generation, coupled with realistic assessment of a congregation's ability to respond to their needs. This is at the heart of this system: unless we truly know and understand the needs of newcomers, we cannot map the best ways to attract and welcome them.

Attracting Newcomers

Every day, we meet people who do not attend church regularly, or at all. Part of the pleasure of reaching out to others includes reawakening the joys that congregational life provides, individually and collectively. A natural part of this process is the desire to share that special quality with others.

You can't be welcoming to people who aren't there, and planning to be welcoming *if* they come is short-sighted. A proactive congregation does not wait until newcomers show up; it reaches out and invites them in. The process is variously called outreach, or evangelism, or communicating; however you name it, it's marketing—a term many church folks prefer to avoid. Marketing means using the tools that best help you get the good news out to a waiting world. You already engage in marketing—making your presence known—in a variety of ways: on your phone answering system, through print ads in the church section, mailings to your congregation, newsletters, and the sign outside your church building; through press releases, direct mailings, the Yellow Pages, flyers, your Web page, and e-mail. The issue is not whether your congregation does marketing—you do, and you will. The issue is whether you do it *well*.

Your Potent Secret Weapon

If you had a secret weapon that could dramatically increase the number of first-time visitors, would you use it? Well, you already have it: your congregation itself. You can increase your visitor-to-regular-attender ratio simply by urging each member to invite friends, neighbors, relatives, and work associates, to join in worship or in some other spiritual or social function of the congregation. Research underscores the power of personal invitation as the best way to encourage visitors to your congregation.

Some denominations run beautifully produced generic TV ads in strategically chosen market areas, hoping that in combination with personal invitation the ads will produce a significant response. The problem lies not in the ads but in the second half of the equation. People are generally hesitant to initiate this kind of invitation, even when the pastor makes a specific request. Many value their own privacy and feel they may be intruding into someone's personal space if they tell others about their relationship with God or about their community of faith. The problem, then, is overcoming this reticence.

Special Events and Big Sundays

An effective way to relieve this shyness is to sponsor congregation-wide outreach events that combine personal invitation with other marketing tactics:

Newspaper publicity and advertising

Press release

Public service announcement

Public access radio or TV

Direct mail

Signs

The Internet

E-mail

Newspaper insert flyer

The purpose is to have the opportunity to tell others about the good things that can happen in their lives through your congregation. When visitors come, as they will, you are then prepared to give them information, through the service program, in brochures, and through a video loop at the fellowship hour depicting congregational activities.

Special events are really ministry opportunities designed to appeal to a specific constituency by addressing some felt need. These events can be on any day of the week and include workshops, seminars, noted speakers, visual arts festivals, social functions, or any activity that meets the needs of a targeted group. A corollary to this is that you must also offer some form of follow-up—such as small-group discussion, a class, or a social activity—to give visitors a reason to return and get to know your congregation in depth. (An example of a special event, "Friendship Sunday," is included at the end of this chapter.)

Two religious holy days, Christmas and Easter, are by their very nature special events. Surprisingly, many congregations fail to take strategic advantage of these two days. They are a golden opportunity to share your spiritual DNA by specifically inviting visitors to participate in planned activity.

Big Sundays as special events are almost always a hit. Genesis Church in the Silicon Valley is a new-start Afrocentric congregation—"a place for new beginnings"—founded some four years ago by pastor Junius Boyd Dotson. He's a Gen-Xer, and he has attracted hundreds of other Gen-Xers and Baby Boomers to his congregation. About every three months, they produce a thematic Big Sunday event. Sometimes the themes are related to special days: Mother's Day, Children's Sunday, a day celebrating African-American heritage, or a day to celebrate the congregation's ministry. As an example, their annual Festival Sunday is the kick-off for the fall season. An inspiring worship service, special music, a nicely produced program, a booklet of upcoming activities, the pastor's stirring message, and children's ministry activities have been important since the founding of the congregation, and even more so on these Big Sundays. Genesis excels in the bountiful spiritual feast it sets out on these days (with the added ingredients of fellowship and good food).

The result? The congregation is committed to high quality in all that it does, so the Genesis folks are quite willing to invite people to these Sundays. Attendance peaks; many newcomers return in succeeding weeks, and some eventually affiliate with this dynamic congregation. It's not the beauty of the building that attracts them; they worship in the gym of a middle school. People come because the members are excited about their life in God, and they want to share the power of God's love with others.

Visitor-Friendly Welcoming

We've noted that congregations like to think of the church building as their home, the place where the "family" gathers for worship and fellowship. The challenge of thinking in these terms is that the building becomes equated with a residence, where only the family is truly welcomed. This is often what plays out in many congregations on Sunday morning; the family gathers, and if there happen to be strangers in their midst, well. . . .

How you imagine your congregation to be affects the way you invite in and welcome newcomers. Chapter Fifty-Three of the Rule of St. Benedict says: "All guests who present themselves are to be welcomed as Christ who said 'I was a stranger and you welcomed me.' Proper honor must be shown to all. . . ." Romans 15:7 says, "So reach out and welcome one another to God's glory. Jesus did it; now *you* do it!" (TM)

When Solomon dedicated the Temple in Jerusalem (1 Kings 8), he prayed not only that it might be a house of prayer for the people of Israel but also that it would be a temple for all peoples. Is your congregation a private home, where only members are welcome, or is it a public temple, where everyone is welcome?

Arch Street Church is a good example of a welcoming temple for all people. It's located in downtown Philadelphia. Street people hang around the church steps, and adult video shops are just a brief walk away, so the environment doesn't seem very welcoming. But this congregation was able to make lemonade out of lemons. Hosts meet people as soon as they enter the building. They ask "Where are you from?" and "What brings you here today?" This information is relayed to the pastor who takes these conversational gambits a bit further by extending a cordial welcome to visitors in noting where they came from. For example, "We want to welcome two guests this morning. They're from San Francisco and are in our city on business." No names are given, no embarrassing requests to stand up are made, but visitors—the authors, in this case—felt very welcome.

The parking situation at Arch Street is a real lemon: they have none, and the City of Brotherly Love issues parking violations seven days a week. The congregation, however, worked out a deal with the city that any automobile displaying a dated dashboard notice from the church (available in the entry area) would not be ticketed. On top of that, the congregation guarantees to pay the fine if, by some remote chance, a ticket is issued. This congregation understands the role that welcoming plays in renewal and growth.

Let's now look at a few basic tactics you can use to create a welcoming atmosphere in your temple for all people.

Make a Good First Impression

It's a cliché, but true: you only get one chance to make a good first impression. The building and grounds of a small nondenominational church showed advanced signs of deferred maintenance. The flowerbeds had more weeds than blooms, and bits of litter were scattered about. The concrete walkway was cracked and slightly buckled, and paint was peeling on window frames. As visitors to the church, we noticed all that immediately. But when we asked the leadership what they could do to make their property more inviting, they never mentioned taking care of the neglect. Over time, they had become oblivious to it.

We asked them to take a clipboard, walk around, and do a ten-minute survey of their grounds from the perspective of a person viewing them for the first time. With a bit of prompting from us, they were taken aback at what they observed as they went through the exercise with "fresh eyes." They quickly mobilized for action. Once they began the clean-up project, they were inspired to do more. They installed an outdoor fountain and placed park benches around it. They laid out and planted new flowerbeds and replaced the walkway. None of these tasks required large sums of money, but they generated great dividends. The property's new look netted the congregation favorable comments not just from visitors but even from people who lived and worked in the area.

Make Your Church Sign Stand Out

Your church signs have three purposes: (1) to identify your church and denomination, (2) to describe your services and activities, and (3) to provide directions. Outdoor signs are meant to be seen, so they should be situated in such a way that they can be read from both directions. Since more people drive by than walk by most churches, your signs should be in the driver's line of sight. They should stand out from other signs in the area and should be large enough to be seen from a reasonable distance. Be brave—paint your signs in bright colors. We've seen too many signs that blend in with the landscaping so well as to be hardly visible. If your congregation is in an out-of-the-way location, purchase portable tent signs and place them in strategic locations about an hour before service time.

Don't neglect your interior signs. Can a first-time visitor easily find the restrooms? Can parents with young children find the nursery or the Sunday school rooms without having to ask? Is the location of the fellowship (coffee hour) area plainly marked? Can a newcomer find the classrooms?

Your Parking Lot Can Be a Welcoming Place

Set aside an area, close to the main entrance, with spaces clearly marked for visitors. If pastor, staff, or key leaders are used to staking out the best places, they'll be happy to give them to newcomers. Assign a host to welcome and distribute worship programs to people on their way from the parking lot to the church. On rainy days, make umbrellas available in the parking lot (some congregations print their logo on them) for the walk from the car to the entrance and back. If your lot is large, parking attendants may be necessary.

How many spaces should be reserved for first-time visitors? What's your average number of visitors at your main service? If it's ten, then set aside that many spaces. You can always increase the number of spaces as the number of first-time visitors increases. (Even if all spaces are taken, newcomers appreciate the fact that you cared enough to provide them.) A Lutheran church has only street parking, yet the members understand the necessity of providing spaces for visitors. They created portable signs marked "Reserved for First-Time Visitors," placed them curbside thirty minutes before service time, and removed them thirty minutes after the start of the service.

Have Welcoming Hosts

Consider rethinking your welcoming process by substituting "hosts" for ushers and greeters. This is more than a change of term. Ushers and greeters often assume that their only responsibility is to extend a friendly welcome when a visitor arrives. Hosts—who should be on duty at key locations—understand that their responsibility extends past a friendly greeting. Hosts are responsible for seeing to it that guests feel welcome, have an opportunity to meet others, and leave feeling good about your congregation.

Give Your Guests Some Space

Your guests want to feel welcome, but they don't expect to be (or want to be) embarrassed by being put through the welcoming hoops that some congregations—among them, maybe yours—have devised. Linda Wiberg, United Methodist minister and California-Nevada conference director of Connectional Ministries, refers to this overly aggressive approach as "vampire evangelism," with its overly aggressive handshake at the door, newcomers being followed from the door to the sanctuary to be sure they sign the guest book, sticking a name tag on them, and on and on and on.

In their zeal to acknowledge visitors, congregations often go overboard by asking them to stand up and identify themselves. If anyone should stand up and be identified, it should be those specially trained people we've just mentioned who can be of assistance or answer questions. Newcomers don't like to be singled out; that's one of the reasons they feel more comfortable visiting larger churches, where they can be relatively anonymous. Getting up and speaking in public is a real fear for many North Americans, so people need to feel some sort of bond with you before they are willing to express themselves publicly.

There are always exceptions, of course, but in general most guests prefer a measure of anonymity so they can observe you and see how you walk your talk as a community of faith. Remember that many are church shopping, looking for information about your community of faith.

At some point in the worship service, visitors should be given a brief and sincere welcome. Where this occurs is not important. As we mentioned in the Preface, for twenty-seven years George Regas issued the same greeting: "Whoever you are, and wherever you are on your journey of faith, you are welcome in this place." As a result of hearing this greeting and sensing its sincerity, the authors and hundreds of others have been attracted to this congregation. We were so moved by it that for the past decade we have mentioned this greeting in our work, and we're happy to note that a large majority of those congregations quickly adopt it, or some version of it, as their own. We believe that its very simplicity and sincerity is the key. It speaks directly to the spiritual seeker. It acknowledges that we may be at different places on a spiritual journey, but all are welcome.

Don't Ask Visitors to Make an Offering

Newcomers often feel that congregations are too much concerned with their own needs—primarily money—and too little concerned with people's needs. To diffuse this feeling, at the time of the offering we suggest that you say, "The offering is a time when those of us who feel moved by God to do so give of our resources. First-time visitors, we're glad you're here; your giving is not required." Thus the newcomer has heard—possibly for the first time—that there are responsibilities in being connected with your congregation, one of which is supporting it financially.

There is one more part to this. The newcomer has probably followed the other liturgical traditions you observe: standing to sing, greeting others at the passing of the peace, or kneeling. The offering is a tactile action; take the plate, place something in it, pass it on. Though you have excused newcomers from the money transaction, they can still participate in the tactile action if you request them, ahead of time, to fill out a communication card.

Communication cards serve the needs of newcomers, regular attenders, and your pastoral obligation to know what's happening in people's lives. These cards let newcomers know that you will pray for them and for their specific needs. It allows regulars to communicate with you, and to indicate their prayer requests or their joys and concerns. Encourage everyone to fill one out and give them time to do it during the service. In addition to praying for God's people, you gain vital statistical information for follow-up.

Adding a gift offer (devotional magazine, special audiocassette, or freshly baked bread) increases the probability of the card being filled out. If newcomers are willing to give you their name, address, and phone number, they are signaling you that they'd like some attention. Exhibit 3.1 shows a typical card.

Establish an "Aisle Ministry"

Visitors report that even a congregation that bends over backward to welcome them at the door often fails to continue welcoming them immediately *after* the service. Members are usually so busy chatting with their friends that it's easy to overlook newcomers. We suggest a simple but effective remedy. Establish an "aisle ministry" of *trained* hosts who are assigned a section or quadrant of the sanctuary. Their

Exhibit 3.1. Sample Communication Card

Welcome to Our Church!

Name _____   Date _____

Address _____

City _____   State _____   Zip code _____

Phone: home (___) _____   work (___) _____

E-mail _____   Fax (___) _____

This is my _____ first _____ second _____ third _____ fourth time here

(or) I'm a regular attender. _____

I have _____ children. (Ages: _____)

☐ I have a prayer request: _____
☐ Please add me/us to your mailing list.
☐ Please contact me/us about the activities checked:
☐ [Church activity #1]   ☐ [Church activity #3]
☐ [Church activity #2]   ☐ [Church activity #4]

We ask you to fill out this card and place it in the offering basket with your financial contribution. If you're a first-time visitor, your presence with us is your contribution for today. Thank you for being with us, and please plan on returning.

---

sole task is to identify newcomers within their section or quadrant, assist them with information, offer to take them or direct them to the coffee hour, and introduce them to at least one or two others.

Make Coffee Hour a Positive Experience

You can destroy every positive impression you have made if you leave a newcomer standing alone during the coffee hour—even for a short time. Trained hosts are especially effective in this situation.

They should introduce themselves, and if possible introduce the newcomer to someone who might share a common interest. For example, introduce a couple with children to similar families, or to a Sunday school teacher.

Another way to alleviate the coffee-hour blues is to run a short introductory video on the life of the church. If it is formatted as a continuous loop, you can let it run during the fellowship time. The video doesn't have to be professionally produced, but it shouldn't look like a home movie, either. A congregational member who knows how to use a video camera could probably do the taping and editing.

Vary the contents; combine still shots and action shots; avoid too many talking heads. Plan it carefully, and script it to be informative and visually pleasing. Keep interviews short (about thirty seconds) and interesting. In your planning, consider these questions:

- How best can we visually portray who we are as a community of faith?

- Which activities are a must for our video?

- Who should be included in the video? Why?

Offer an Information Center

Newcomers should have access to adequate information about the congregation, but let them make their own choices. An information center might be as simple as a table, or it might be a booth or kiosk. Locate them in all high-traffic areas, and at all key entrances, where newcomers and others can (1) pick up literature, (2) learn about upcoming events, and (3) sign up for events. Include current and back issues of denominational and devotional publications clearly labeled "Free." You might also offer a free audiocassette with a specially prepared welcoming message.

One congregation insisted that these tables be staffed. Unfortunately, the volunteers, all good-hearted individuals, had a tendency to push information on people and drive them away. We suggested that the congregation try a test: for two months, continue as usual with the staffed tables. For another two months, simply lay out a wide array of information on unstaffed tables and let people choose what they want. For both tests, they were to keep a count of literature they put on the table and then recount what was left after the service. They were surprised to discover that people picked up more literature during the unstaffed months, when people could decide for themselves what they wanted to know.

No One Form of Liturgy Fits All

Tastes in liturgy vary enormously, and people are spiritually fed in a variety of ways. The issue isn't which is the best type of worship, but which type is authentic and appropriate for your congregation and for those you are called to serve. Increasingly, though, the trend is toward experiential worship that sees the sacred in every aspect of life, and where "smells and bells," multimedia, drama, and dance enhance these experiences. *Religion Watch* (April 1999) notes that multisensory forms of worship are being rediscovered. There is a new appreciation of liturgical worship; "churches are returning to the 'old' and using guided meditative prayer . . . incense, candles and historical Christian rituals."

Time

The proper hour for a worship service is whatever hour is most convenient for the majority of your target audience. For example, the tradition of 11:00 A.M. Sunday worship developed in response to the needs of a constituency (typically, an agrarian community). Today, hours of worship can accommodate people's changing needs for free time with family and friends. Sausalito Presbyterian Church in California holds its service at 9:00 A.M. and attracts a large congregation. Seattle's St. Mark's Episcopal Cathedral provides a late-night worship experience, Sundays at 10:00 P.M., where hundreds gather in a candlelight atmosphere to worship according to the ancient monastic service of Compline.

Music

The type of music you use should grow out of the needs of the congregation and its identity. Thus, a particular style of music should not be used simply because the congregation thinks it will help it grow. The style employed should reflect the spiritual DNA of the congregation. Why? Because as Rick Warren writes in *The Purpose-Driven Church*, "The music you choose 'positions' your church in your community. It defines who you are. Once you decide on the style of music you're going to use in worship, you have set the direction of your church in far more ways than you realize. It will determine the kind of people you attract, the kind of people you keep, and the kind of people you lose." The message of God's transforming love can be conveyed through many styles of music.

Preaching

Messages aimed at reaching newcomers should address a need, and be filled with fresh facts and ideas that offer a solution to problems occurring in everyday life, undergirded by scripture. Topical messages are effective in motivating people to continue attending. An outline of the message with scripture references, as well as fill-in-the-blank sentences on major points, might be distributed to each person in attendance. These not only keep their attention but are also a handy take-home reference tool. To attract visitors back, publish message titles well in advance.

Announcements

Make your verbal announcements clear, concise, and brief. We once attended a worship service in which the announcements consumed seventeen minutes of service time. The intention was to empower the congregation with information; the net result was sheer boredom. Who can remember that many announcements? Restrict them to activities to which everyone present at the service is invited; print all others in the program. Also, avoid talking about money during the service. Remember what we said about newcomers and money? Negative financial reports may give an incorrect impression to newcomers. What's the solution? Send out special financial mailings intended only for incorporated members. The exception would be a brief announcement or short testimonial on Sundays during your stewardship campaign, though even this is chancy. We recall seeing a cartoon of a church's notice board. The message read, "This is Stewardship Sunday. Visitors, please come back next week."

Drama, Visuals, and Videos

Baby Boomers, Gen-Xers, and especially Millennials are the first generations raised in a technological culture. They are visually oriented, and indications are that the generations following will be even more tied to visual and dramatic presentation. Projecting images and words to songs on a large screen can be an effective enhancement to worship. There is revived interest in the Western church for using three-to-five-minute dramas to present stories of faith in new and innovative ways. A video presentation creates impact, integrates the element of surprise in a service, and can be used to illustrate a vision or a need effectively. In-house infomercials using Microsoft PowerPoint can enhance one's receptivity to the announcement. A Baptist church sketches out its videotape announcements in advance, and on Friday evenings young people assemble in the sanctuary to videotape the sketch for presentation on Sunday morning.

Remember to Follow Up

Your congregation should be proactive in following up on a newcomer's visits. Why? Because the odds are stacked against you. Sixty percent of your first-time visitors will not return. Forty percent consider returning if their first visit is a good experience for them. You need to contact those who show some interest via an *intentional* follow-up and response system. Here are a few ideas.

Door-to-Door Contact

Some congregations prefer face-to-face follow-up. Whether it is appropriate or not depends on community standards. Certainly, some people welcome such a visit, while others may feel it is an unwarranted and unwanted intrusion. It's always best to notify people that you will be coming *before* you ring their doorbell. Keep your visit short.

Phone Contact Follow-Up

We believe that a follow-up should be as professional as you can make it within the confines of your time, talent, and treasure.

Form a ministry team, write scripts, and then rehearse a phone follow-up. Two scripts might be devised: one for live calls, and one for answering machine messages. This would be a useful exercise for a volunteer training session. A script or an outline keeps the volunteer "on purpose." Consider some of the telemarketing calls you get that sound as if the person was handed a script a few seconds before calling. You don't want your volunteers to sound like that. Phone call role-playing quickly indicates who should make these calls.

Phone contacts should be brief—a thank-you for visiting. Did the newcomer have a pleasant experience? Are there any questions about the congregation? Does the person have a prayer request? End with the hope that he or she will consider visiting again in the near future.

Reaching a live person is, of course, optimal, but electronic communications are an integral part of today's world, so leaving a short message on a machine is acceptable. The important point is that you made an attempt to contact the visitor. You can also accomplish the same thing through an e-mail contact.

Call to First-Time Visitor

Visitor return rate is greatly influenced by the length of time that elapses between a visit to the congregation and the follow-up contact. To be effective, the contact should be made within forty-eight hours. After that time, the visitor return rate drops dramatically.

Sunday afternoon is the best time for follow-up. Monday is second best. Tuesday is third best.

Second- and Third-Time Visit

Second- and third-time visits are even more important. A contact should be called within a few days of his or her visit. A person who expresses a level of interest in the congregation should be invited to a scheduled newcomer orientation meeting.

Written Follow-Up

A written follow-up is appropriate after each of the first three visits. Newcomers appreciate hearing from the congregation. This could range from a handwritten note from the pastor to a personal comment written on a form letter.

These are a just a few basic ideas on how you can turn your congregation from a private home into a public temple for all people. These and the tactics listed in the Welcoming Quotient (WQ) survey in Chapter Seven (Exhibit 7.2) are ways to strengthen a particular system in the body of Christ.

An Example of a Special Event

*Friendship Sunday: Get the Whole Congregation
Involved*
Friendship Sunday is a special event that focuses on inviting and welcoming newcomers. The key to its success is the intentional participation by the congregation.

Friendship Sunday is much like an introduction to a significant aspect of your congregation's life. This is a special day, a joyous celebration of who you and your visitors are—the people of God gathered together. Friendship Sunday is a day to celebrate relationships in many forms:

- Relationship with God
- Relationships developed in your community of faith
- Relationships with those not part of your congregation

It is a day to share what initially attracted you and others to the congregation:

- Worship, music, and preaching
- Small groups
- Opportunities for education and fellowship

Procedure. In the first mailing, a letter goes out to everyone on the church's mailing list, in which the pastor explains the purpose of the event. The second mailing includes another letter from the pastor and a specially prepared Friendship Sunday Packet, containing:

- A *Friendship Sunday Invitations List* with spaces for six names, addresses, and phone numbers
- Six preprinted invitations
- Six envelopes
- Six stamps

Regular attenders are first asked to create their own "invitations list" of six people (relatives, friends, neighbors, and so on). Then they are asked to personalize the invitations as an added encouragement to the recipients. Finally, they drop the invitations in the mail at least two weeks prior to the date of Friendship Sunday.

The invitations lists are then turned in to the church office so invitees who come to Friendship Sunday can be acknowledged by mail. The lists are also used to create a database for possible future contact.

An Alternative Approach. Host a Sunday brunch. Make available a supply of Friendship Sunday materials, including postage stamps. As part of the brunch, invite members to address and personalize their invitations. You achieve two goals: provide a fellowship activity, and get the invitations addressed and mailed.

Collect the completed invitation list forms for data input.

Exhibit 3.2. Twelve-Week Time Line for Friendship Sunday and Other Special Events

Twelve Weeks Before the Event

What is the mission of this event?

List your goals and objectives for this Sunday.

Identify and recruit your support personnel.

Establish liaison responsibilities:

- Who will act as liaison with the pastor?
- With the music director?
- With the hospitality or fellowship committee?
- With the ushers and greeters?
- With office administrative or clerical staff?

Ten or Nine Weeks Before the Event

Start on your brochure or welcome packet.

Start working on your Sunday program.

Start working on the publicity pieces:

- PR (public relations) press release for local or neighborhood newspapers
- Invitation or mailer you will use
- Letter from the pastor to church leaders
- Letter from pastor to parishioners
- Announcement for Sunday programs
- Advertising copy for signs, posters, flyers, banners

Create announcement board materials.

(Continued)

Exhibit 3.2. Continued

Eight Weeks Before the Event

Write progress reports from the ministry team in regard to their liaison responsibilities.

Complete any PR or publicity pieces.

Arrange for printing and preparation of signage.

Seven or Six Weeks Before the Event

Pick up and check all printing, signage, etc.

Mail pastor's letter to church leaders.

Give or send flyer to parishioners regarding the event.

Include an Invitation Form for names and addresses of prospects they feel should be invited.

Four Weeks Before the Event

Place announcement in Sunday program.

Mail pastor's letter to parishioners.

Begin lists of prospects' names and addresses.

Begin computer input of mailing list.

Three Weeks Before the Event

Place announcement in Sunday program.

Complete gathering of lists of prospects.

Complete computer input of mailing list.

Send out invitations to prospects.

Two Weeks Before the Event

Place announcement in Sunday program.

Include a pep talk during the service about the total number of prospects who have been invited.

Send out PR materials.

Place advertisement.

Check and print special event or program bulletin.

One Week Before the Event

Complete welcoming materials.

Place announcement in Sunday program.

Urge parishioners to contact prospects to confirm attendance. (This helps in planning seating.)

Review procedures with hosts, hospitality committee, etc.

Arrange for flowers.

Conduct special cleaning of worship space, restrooms, children's rooms, parking lot, and church grounds.

Check the special printed program.

Meet to review final procedures.

Day of the Special Event or Sunday

Welcome guests, give them welcome brochures and packets; ushers provide programs.

Service focuses on friends and relationships—what your congregation has to offer.

Members accompany their guests to the coffee hour and introduce them.

During the Week Following the Event

Within forty-eight hours, lay members call visitors.

Pastor sends thank-you letters.

Evaluate strengths and weaknesses of the event.

Recognize and thank all who worked on event.

Two to Four Weeks After the Event

All return visitors should be contacted and invited to a church activity.

A Warm Welcome to All Who Enter

In summary, your congregation should make it its business to be welcoming to all people who pass through the doors. Realistically, however, no congregation can serve all people's needs with the same degree of quality. Each congregation must think of the welcoming as more than making newcomers feel at home.

The welcoming system is rooted in a strategic decision: a desire to share your very being, your identity, with others—a decision of breathtaking proportions that includes sharing spiritual intimacy and vulnerability. The welcoming system invites you to go beyond simply making nice, to the next level: inclusion in the life and work of the congregation.

4

We're Here to Care
Your Nurturing System

In *After Many a Summer Dies the Swan*, Aldous Huxley describes a conversation about the reality of eternity—God. Jeremy questions that eternity is a reality. Propter replies that eternity is real for all who fulfill the conditions under which it can be experienced. Jeremy inquires why anyone would want to fulfill them. Propter replies, "Why should anyone choose to go to Athens to see the Parthenon? Because it's worth the bother. And the same is true of eternity. The experience of timeless good is worth all the trouble it involves." "Timeless good," Jeremy retorts; "I don't know what the word means." "Why should you?" says Propter; "you've never bought your ticket to Athens."

Congregations and individuals are ticket holders. The ticket for the individual is a commitment—whether by baptism, confirmation, membership, or regular attendance—to discipleship and participation in your community of faith. However, before investing in a ticket, the individual asks, "Can I grow spiritually in this place?" For the congregation, the question is quite different: "How can we effectively incorporate the newcomer, yet sustain the faith of existing congregants?" The answer to both questions is found in one word: *nurture*.

Nurturing is caring. It is through caring that discipleship is introduced to newcomers. It is the process that moves people toward the center of the life and work of the congregation through deepening

their connectedness to God and to each other. It is about really caring for each other, and developing ways to express that caring to
others.

Author-commentator Bill Moyers says that the search for spirituality is not the story of just the last decade, but of the century.
It is part and parcel of the story of people on a spiritual journey to
find meaning in their lives that only a relationship with God can
provide. Creating an environment that supports that relationship
begins with how people are welcomed at the worship celebration.
In fact, the entry point for a large number of people is the front
door of worship; for most congregations it is here that nurturing
begins. As necessary as the Sunday worship celebration is, it is not
enough to support the full spiritual growth of the individual; nor
does it ensure the growth of your congregation. Growth comes
when people find ways to deepen their spiritual life. Going deeper
happens when a congregation is intentional about maintaining a
nurturing environment in which one can grow, when it offers a way
to buy a ticket.

The Angel Says "Grow, Grow"

This connectedness of nurture and growth is found throughout
scripture and in other sacred writings. The Talmud, for example,
says, "Every blade of grass has its angel that bends over it and whis-
pers, 'Grow, grow!'" In Mark 4:3–8, Jesus tells the story of the farmer
who scatters seeds for a new crop. Seeds that fall on rocky ground
can't take root and wither. Seeds that fall on fertile ground—ground
that can nurture and support growth—prosper and "produce thirty
or sixty or even a hundred times as much as was planted." Jesus then
extends his analogy to people. Those without roots make no lasting connections, while those in a healthy environment bloom
where they are planted. Growth, in the right environment, is
inevitable; living things grow best in a loving, caring, environment.
Intentional nurture creates an atmosphere of acceptance and results
in people being incorporated into the life of a spiritual community.

As one of the four key systems in the body of Christ, nurturing is vital, for it is through this system that:

- People feel they belong

- They feel appreciated

- They feel cared for

The welcoming system relates to attracting people to your congregation. A healthy nurturing system keeps them coming back, and once they are incorporated it keeps them committed:

- Willing to awaken to the presence of God in their lives

- Able to explore their faith questions

- Likely to feel safe in this exploration

The congregation enjoys benefits, too:

- More people are attracted and fewer leave.

- Nurtured people are likely to give of their time, talent, and treasure.

- Seeing results in their own lives, nurtured people are inspired to serve others.

- Individuals and families are strengthened through sharing and relationship building with others they meet on the journey.

- Nurtured people are inclined to invite others into congregational participation.

Nurturing 24/7/365

With benefits like these, why doesn't every congregation stress the importance of nurture, especially in view of the fact that anyone— long-term member, new member, regular attender—who feels lack of caring is a potential dropout? Up to one-third of all current members in a congregation at a given time say they do not feel they are truly part of the community of faith. There are many reasons, of course, but primarily people leave because they don't feel cared for; or they don't make lasting friendships; or they aren't able to find their particular place in the life of the congregation to exercise their gifts and talents, or ways to explore their spirituality. Because of its importance, nurture is a key system that must be kept active on a 24/7/365 basis: twenty-four hours a day, seven days a week, 365 days a year. It must be ongoing, sustainable, authentic to the community of faith, and able to respond to people's needs naturally and in the moment.

Before Warner Brown was elected to the United Methodist episcopate for the Denver area in 2000, we had the privilege of working with him and his congregation. They maintain a large facility—sanctuary, chapel, meeting rooms, social hall, classroom buildings—facing a grassy quadrangle. As we were in the midst of making a point about the necessity of listening, some young skateboarders noisily glided by the windows. Although this had been a problem for the congregation, the configuration of the facility is ideal for skateboarding. Chasing them away had become part of the regular routine, but it didn't work—the kids just kept coming back.

A few of those at the meeting were upset with the kids for violating their space and wanted something done. Bishop Brown said, "We've just been talking about listening; let's do some, shall we?" He went outside and spoke to the skateboarders for a few minutes and returned with them in tow—eight young boys, skateboards and all. He asked the folks in the room to welcome them; they did with somewhat grudging applause. The bishop invited them to sit down and asked someone to bring them refreshments—sodas, cookies, and chips.

He said to them, "Boys, we want to listen to you. You know that some of our folks are upset with you for skateboarding on our property. Share with us why you do it." The boys were very forthcoming. They had no adequate place to skateboard, and this church and a neighboring Lutheran church were the best places in the area.

He told them that the congregation was concerned about elderly members getting hurt, and about the damage that the continuous skateboarding had already done to the property. A person in the room asked the boys why they didn't use the designated skateboard area the city had set aside for them. The boys replied that it was near the edge of town, very difficult to get to, and located in an unsafe area. The bishop then said, "Well, we both have a problem. You need a safe place to skateboard, and we need to prevent our facilities from further damage. Why don't we work together to solve both problems and meet our needs?"

Listening leads to caring. The congregation was nurtured as the boys listened and understood their concerns. The boys were nurtured as well by congregants who saw with fresh eyes a need to provide a safe and supporting environment for young people of their community. The boys left, warmed by applause and heartfelt wishes of support. In that potentially chaotic episode, Bishop Brown put into practice the essence of any effective nurturing system: listening to each other in mutual respect as children of God.

Barriers That Prevent Nurture

A number of barriers prevent a congregation from implementing a meaningful nurturing system. Let's look at them and see if they sound familiar.

Not Knowing Who You Are

Your spiritual DNA is your identity. As such, it is the basis for doing what the congregation is called to do. Sometimes the identity is so weak that it is difficult to differentiate a congregation from a social or civic group, or from a club or a sports team. Even though those community organizations make a real contribution to society, their reason for being is not rooted in spiritual identity. Remember our mention of the ABC syndrome—anyplace but the church? If your own members can't distinguish you from a civic or social organization, then naturally they look to other sources for nurture and growth, whether it's in a twelve-step program, a self-help book, or a secular organization that serves people in a less hierarchical, less institutional, less controlled environment.

Not Knowing Why You Exist

The short distance from the head to the heart is often the most difficult journey a congregation can take. If the tendency is to think primarily from an institutional perspective and see your job as building good, solid, active, giving members, then the congregation's primary task is one of maintenance, not transformation. Yet your community of faith has been singled out by God to do what no other organization can do: bring about radical transformation of individuals and society by inviting people into a closer walk with God, and into relationship with others. Only the Church has been given the power and authority to do that, and it cannot happen without nurture.

After years of equating meetings with ministry, committees with community, and reports with relationships, it is painfully evident that a large number of congregations have lost sight of their unique calling. Transformation cannot happen without nurturing. If new members are not effectively nurtured—and feel cared for—they will not grow, but instead drop out. Bill Tully, rector of St. Bartholomew's Church in New York City, reminds us that "people come to church to be touched, to belong." Transformation means touching people in such a positive way that they are never the same again. A powerful mission, with transformation as its primary task, promotes growth for the individual and for the congregation.

Staying Inside the Box

People are nurtured in a variety of ways, and your congregation must be flexible enough to meet people wherever they are on their journey of faith. A congregation may rely heavily on programs. Nurture, however, is a *process*, not a preset program. There is more to nurturing than spirituality in a box. The quest for meaning and for connection often results in questions that are not always clear; even if the questions are clear, the answers may not be. The complexities of the world in which we live, and the challenges we are called on to face, are not easily contained within the confines of a neat and tidy program. This is not an indictment of programs. Use good programs, by all means, but think of them as just one of many ways to nurture individuals. Add creativity, options, and choices that reflect your DNA. Nurture should be as natural to a congregation as breathing is to an individual.

Abandoning New Members

After putting enormous effort into attracting and welcoming newcomers, a congregation might abandon them to shift for themselves after they affiliate. Here's an example. One new member said to us, "I'm tired of filling up their bank account, when they keep leaving my heart on empty." It eventually dawns on these folks that they are there mainly to add statistics to the church rolls and to help pay the bills. This particular congregation does not see its task as providing continuing care. It says, in effect, to new members, "Now it's your turn. Prove yourself, sign up for a committee, and start supporting us financially." It should be asking, "What can we do to support you in your spiritual growth?"

Neglecting to Nurture All Members

Every congregation—including yours—has three "doors," three points of entry or exit. Most people first encounter your community of faith, as we said earlier, through the front door of Sunday worship. Others come in through the side door of small groups, classes, activities, and events. It's enjoyable to watch regular attenders and newcomers enter through the front door, and it's a source of pleasure to know that the side door is open for other activities. But it's the third door—the back door—that's the most problematic.

The back door is invisible to the fully incorporated, but wide open to those who feel some degree of alienation. This door is rarely monitored; it needs some kind of spiritual alarm system to signal you when someone is contemplating leaving your congregation. It's fairly easy to predict that new members who do not feel nurtured and are not fully incorporated are likely to exit in about twelve months. Even long-term members will pass through the back door quietly and unobtrusively if they are not nurtured. A good nurturing system keeps that back door locked by offering the ongoing means of spiritual growth.

Personal Commitment

People are increasingly wary of committing themselves. Partly this is time-related; we have fewer discretionary hours than we used to have. Many feel they don't have enough time to handle their personal, family, and business obligations, so getting involved in a community of faith is seen as an added burden. Yet we're also in a time of instant gratification, when people want all the benefits right now, but few of the responsibilities.

Both of these factors mitigate against commitment. Unwillingness to commit to a single congregation is further complicated by the idea that one can look to several congregations as a spiritual home for oneself and one's family. We hear, "I don't need to commit to any one church." For many, a congregation becomes a theater they go to witness a performance, rather than the nurturing place it is intended to be. The message is abundantly clear: a better job of supporting others in their spiritual growth is essential.

Spirituality Comes in Many Shapes and Sizes

"No one size fits all" is a concept that we hammer away at to underscore that people cannot be slotted into a single approach. We saw an excellent example of this concept during a consultation in Edmonton, Alberta, Canada. A church member who had great pride in his city made several recommendations about what to see while we were there. He directed us to the Provincial Museum, which was hosting a special exhibit, "Anno Domini: Jesus Through the Centuries—Exploring the Heart of Two Millennia."

Its purpose, the catalogue stated, was to "glimpse some of the ways Jesus has been understood and how this understanding has shaped and reshaped culture." Entering the exhibit area, we stood before a curved wall with the question, "Who do you say that I am?" emblazoned in large letters. Surrounding the question were short answers, including Savior, Rabbi, Teacher, Poet, Cosmic Christ, King of Kings, and Son of Man. The exhibit focused on presenting the answers to the question while retaining the centrality of the person of Jesus.

A video presentation based on the Beatitudes used television and film clips to portray how Jesus has the ability to speak to us about the realities of life—the joys, the sorrows, the tragedies, the horrors—that often confront us. Each of eighteen aspects of Jesus was displayed in its own space and with its own theme. Among them were: "Turning Point of History," "King of Kings," "Cosmic Christ," "Son of Man," "The Universal Man," "Prince of Peace," "Teacher of Common Sense," "Liberator," and "Man Who Belongs to the World." Each display was a snapshot of him, with pictures of how people find nurture through images of Jesus. Each display featured ancient and contemporary works of art and artifacts, with contemporary and ancient quotations.

Along with the other visitors—many of whom were from other religious traditions—we were shown a variety of ways in which artists and others experienced Jesus. We suspect that most of the visitors had already been exposed to a single view of Jesus. When they found a particular area of the exhibit that best fit their picture, they felt very comfortable, but probably not so comfortable in other areas.

We listened carefully to people's comments. A woman was thrilled over the King of Kings display, another with the concept of Jesus as Cosmic Christ. Several people found Jesus the Teacher of Common Sense to be their favorite model. Still others rejoiced at the display of Jesus the Prince of Peace image. A couple were standing close by. The man said, "I never realized that there were so many ways to see Jesus."

His wife commented, "It's like there's one Jesus, but so many faces of him." As people worked their way through the exhibit they, indeed, saw at least eighteen ways to experience Jesus. The sacred can come to us in many forms, any one of which can nurture our spiritual growth.

Where Are You on the Spirituality Wheel?

Corinne Ware, in her book *Discover Your Spiritual Type*, observes that people experience God in a variety of ways. A professor at the Seminary of the Southwest, Ware has extended the spirituality typology developed by the late Urban Holmes to help people understand why they don't feel they fit a particular worship style. Ware suggests that understanding one's spiritual type can promote growth both for the individual and the worshiping community alike. To do this, she developed a Spirituality Wheel—a "selector for spiritual type"—to explain how and why we grow spiritually in various religious environments. The Spirituality Wheel (Figure 4.1) is not intended as an exclusive indicator of how one connects with God; rather, it's an indicator of one's preferences. The wheel itself is a

Figure 4.1. The Spirituality Wheel

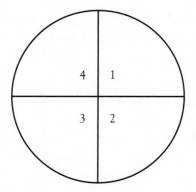

Source: Reprinted from *Discover Your Spiritual Type: A Guide to Individual and Congregational Growth*, by Corinne Ware, with permission.

simple design, a circle divided into four quadrants to fit her thesis that there are essentially four spiritual types. Let's take a brief look at each one before describing how to find one's spiritual type.

Type One: Spirituality of the Head

People of the first type focus on an intellectual exploration of what they perceive to be the real world, the concrete world of daily life. This type can be expressed in any number of ways, from a clearly delineated theological viewpoint to study groups and intellectually stimulating sermons. People of this type are often structured and orderly and draw inspiration from words, including written prayers.

Type Two: Spirituality of the Heart

This type is characterized by richness of feeling and the ability to experience God in the moment. Many of the fastest-growing congregations in the United States express this spirituality with emphasis on a personal relationship with God present in the here and now. The heart types depend on getting their information more from the feeling state than from the factual information they receive (as do types one and four). This type is characterized by an affective approach to ministry that finds God more in the heart than in the mind.

Type Three: Mystic Spirituality

People in this type are on a spiritual quest, a journey to experience the reality of God. This type finds power in silence and in just being. Many popular inspirational books, such as Thomas Moore's *Care of the Soul* and Donald Walsh's *Conversations with God*, are representative of this type. Type three sees the interior world as the real world and responds to meditation, retreats, and periods of silence away from the busyness of daily life.

Type Four: Kingdom Spirituality

Ware now calls this fourth type "Crusading Spirituality." This spiritual type stresses commitment to social justice and community needs. It emphasizes helping through social concern and direct action. People of this type tend to be discontent in congregations where they perceive a lack of concern about social issues; among their ranks have been numerous heroic change agents—notably Martin Luther King Jr.

This spirituality emphasizes prophetic ministry and sees God working through each of us to make a better world. Kingdom (Crusading) Spirituality congregations tend to have a clear, though often controversial, public face.

Combinations of Spirituality

The theory of four spiritual types offers a clear indicator that there are many paths to God. Indeed, individuals and congregations frequently have more than one preferred form of spirituality. One type may predominate, but there may also be a strong second preference. Each type has something important to contribute to the whole of one's relationship to God. An individual's or congregation's Spirituality Wheel is usually weighted in one quadrant more than the others, though it can be more or less evenly divided. This is not to suggest that there must be a perfect balance in each quadrant. Rather, it is valuable to understand and celebrate the variety of ways in which individuals and congregations experience the sacred. This is how it should be. There are many pathways to God; one size definitely doesn't fit all.

Finding Your Spiritual Type

To discern one's particular type, Ware provides three basic tests: for Protestants (included in this chapter), Roman Catholics, and Jews. Each test contains the same categories; although the questions are similar, they are written to fit the culture and basic theological concepts of the group. She divides the tests into the same twelve categories: order of worship, time, prayer, music, preaching, emphasis, support of causes, criticism, dominating themes, membership criteria, ritual and liturgy, and concept of God (see Exhibit 4.1). Each category has four numbered questions, with one question based on each of the four types.

Exhibit 4.1. Spirituality Type Selector Test

The Order of Worship
1. A carefully planned and orderly worship program is a glory to God.
2. A deeply moving and spontaneous meeting is a glory to God.
3. Simplicity and some silence are important elements needed for worship.
4. It is not a service, but ordering ourselves to God's service, that is important.

Time
1. Stick to announced beginning and ending times for the worship service.
2. It is important to extend the meeting time if one feels led to do so.
3. All time is God's time. A sense of timelessness is important.
4. Gather whenever and for as long as you need in order to accomplish the task.

Prayer
1. Words express poetic praise; we ask for knowledge and guidance.
2. Let words and feelings evoke God's presence in this moment.
3. Empty the mind of distractions and simply BE in the presence of the Holy.
4. My life and my work are my prayer.

Music
1. Music and lyrics express praise to God and belief about God.
2. Singing warms and unites us and expresses the soul's deepest heart.
3. Chant and tone bring the soul to quietness and union with God.
4. Songs can mobilize and inspire to great effort and dedication.

Preaching
1. The Word of God, rightly proclaimed, is the centerpiece of worship.
2. The gospel movingly preached is the power of God to change lives.
3. Proclamation is heard when the Spirit of God speaks to the inward heart.
4. What we do is our "preaching," and it speaks louder than anything we say.

(Continued)

Exhibit 4.1. Continued

Emphasis
1. A central purpose is that we fulfill our vocation (calling) in the world.
2. A central purpose is that we learn to walk in holiness with the Lord.
3. A central purpose is that we be one with the Creator.
4. A central purpose is that we obey God's will completely.

Support of Causes
(If necessary, circle the words that apply and then select the category or categories with the most circles.)

1. Support seminaries, publishing houses, scholarship, and preaching to others.
2. Support evangelism, missions, and spreading the word on television and radio.
3. Support places of retreat, spiritual direction, and liturgical reform.
4. Support political action to establish justice in society and its institutions.

Criticism
1. Sometimes we are (I am) said to be too intellectual, dogmatic, and "dry."
2. Sometimes we are (I am) said to be too emotional, dogmatic, and anti-intellectual.
3. Sometimes we are (I am) said to be escaping from the world and not realistic.
4. Sometimes we are (I am) said to have tunnel vision and be too moralistic.

Dominating Themes
(If necessary, circle the words that apply and then select the category or categories with the most circles.)

1. Discernment, discipline, knowledge, order, grace, justification
2. Love, conversion, witness, spontaneity, sanctification
3. Poverty, humility, wisdom, letting go, transcendence
4. Simplicity, purity of heart, action, temperance, obedience, martyrdom

Membership Criteria

(What the congregation believes is necessary; what you believe is necessary)

1. Assent to doctrine, baptism, and endorsement by the group.
2. A personal inward experience of God, baptism, and public declaration.
3. All who face Godward are incorporated in the Holy.
4. Solidarity with humankind is membership in God's kingdom.

Ritual and Liturgy

1. Ritual and liturgy evoke memory and presence, teaching traditional truths.
2. Liturgy and ritual ceremonies are not of great importance.
3. Ritual and liturgy are ways in which God becomes present to us.
4. Ritual and liturgy are one way we make statements about inner conviction.

Concept of God

1. God is revealed in scripture, sacrament, and Jesus Christ and his cross.
2. I can feel that God is real and that Christ lives in my heart.
3. God is mystery and can be grasped for but not completely known.
4. We participate in the mystery of God when we become cocreators with God in the world.

Source: Reprinted from *Discover Your Spiritual Type: A Guide to Individual and Congregational Growth* by Corinne Ware, with permission from the Alban Institute, Inc., 7315 Wisconsin Avenue, Suite 1250 West, Bethesda, Maryland 20814. Copyright © (1995). All rights reserved.

To take the test, you simply read the questions and choose statements that most nearly correspond to how you experience that concept. You may choose one, none, or more than one statement.

The Spirituality Wheel is then used in conjunction with the test. Starting with the first test question (on order of worship), you draw a simple spoke from the center of the wheel to the outside edge within the quadrant whose number corresponds to the answer(s) you have chosen on the test; if you choose more than one statement, you draw more than one spoke. Continue in the same way for all twelve categories on the test. By counting the number of spokes in each quadrant, you get a picture of your personal preference.

To make the picture of your congregation's preferences complete, have as many members as possible take the test and collate the answers. Then you'll have a detailed portrait of the spiritual types that make up your congregation.

Practical Application of the Wheel

We often use the Spirituality Wheel in our work. Several years ago, we found a powerful example of how it can help a congregation understand itself and nurture others. A church team took the basic test and found that they had a very strong preference for quadrant two, heart spirituality. In fact, more than 75 percent of the team members indicated quadrant two as their preference. We urged them to test this with the congregation as a whole, so for the next three weeks the team gathered responses from about two hundred of their worshiping community. When the results were in, the team saw that the congregants also displayed a strong preference—once again, by more than 75 percent—for quadrant two.

We then asked the team members to look at those activities and programs that moved them to emotion or to richness of feeling. Our reason for requesting this action was that the congregants had a history of conflict among themselves and with a succession of pastors. We suggested to the team that one reason for the conflict might stem from the fact that the congregation did little that reflected their authentic identity. We encouraged the team to create new activities that would embody their newly uncovered quadrant-two nature and then test the activities to determine if they better reflected their identity.

Miracles do happen! Within a few months, the warring factions had settled into an amiable peace as they became united in activities that nurtured their feelings of connectedness to God. Newcomers remarked at the feeling of peace they encountered. The congregation realized a benefit as a substantially larger number of first-time visitors returned. It was able to carry out the mission with efficiency and delight by offering those ministry pathways that reflected its basic spirituality type; the team became willing to stretch by offering other pathways that appealed to other spiritual types. It is only by being willing to nurture people in a variety of ways that discipleship can become a natural, unforced process of growth for individuals and the congregation.

Nurturing Women and Men

Just as there are different types of spirituality, a strong nurturing system must also recognize that men and women respond in their own way to spirituality. Discovering how your congregation can nurture both men and women can be a rewarding path.

Nurturing Women

Though women make up the greater proportion of church members and active volunteers, congregations have not always done a good job of nurturing them. Women are struggling to find forms of spirituality that meet their needs as women. Their struggle is not with the outside world but with their congregations, the very places they expect to provide them peace, guidance, and support. Often given only the two choices of "Martha" (service) and "Mary" (devotion), women have patiently waited for the congregation as a whole to value the many-dimensional facets of their spirituality.

During the Sunday worship service, the pastor introduced us to the congregation as their newly retained consultants. After the service, Lydia van Allen, a longtime and active member, wanted a word with us. She guided us to a quiet room and poured out her story. Her only daughter, now twenty-two, was severely disabled. Caring for her was very difficult, and Lydia was the sole care provider. No matter how tired she was, she had to get up at odd hours during the night. Some nights, she said, she was so exhausted from caring from her daughter that she'd sit down on the stairs to catch her breath. Eventually, these "stair times" became prayer times. "I have a little quiet chat with God, just sitting there on the steps," Lydia said, adding that by finding strength in the process it became a significant part of her daily routine. Then she burst into tears: "I've been praying like this for all these years, but I've never felt that I could tell anyone in our church about it. It isn't appropriate here, you know."

The culture of Lydia's congregation had signaled—perhaps inadvertently—that one doesn't share these very personal experiences. It's not that they weren't people of faith; they were. It's not that they don't pray; they do. But outside of the formal liturgical service, there was no place for individual personal sharing about God. Lydia's worst fear was the reaction of her friends. "They'd think I'm odd," she said, "I don't believe they would understand." With her permission, we shared her story with the leadership. They were shocked that she would feel that way, but on reflection they knew she was right, and they admitted they were often disparaging of "emotionalism." We suggested that they create a forum where people can tell their stories about the power of God's love in their lives, in a safe, nurturing, atmosphere. They took a first tentative step and created a life-sharing group. They later followed up with a faith-sharing group. Lydia's story has dramatically transformed the atmosphere of the congregation.

Feminine Aspects of the Sacred

Whatever their spiritual type, women are going to be involved in the congregation not only as members and active participants but also as leaders. More and more women are in seminaries. Other women have taken the lead in exploring the feminine aspect of the sacred, drawn to different aspects of scripture and sacred writings to discern feminine images of God—for example, the interest in exploring the mysticism of Hildegard of Bingen and Dame Julian of Norwich. There's a budding interest in rediscovering Mary as an archetype of the feminine side of deity. Lauren Artress, a canon of Grace Cathedral in San Francisco, leads "Let's Walk with Mary" encounters. She has also introduced one of the most innovative ways of nurturing people through experiential spirituality: the labyrinth, an ancient form of walking meditation.

Popularizing the Labyrinth

Artress calls this rediscovery "one of the most important spiritual developments of our day. The labyrinth is a tool of self-alignment that can help put our lives in perspective. As we walk a sacred path, we realize that 'we are spiritual beings on a human path, not simply human beings on a spiritual path.'"

The labyrinth has been in use for centuries in many cultures, on many continents. The best-known example is the geometric design that was embedded into the stone floor of the great cathedral at Chartres, France, sometime in the twelfth century. In 1991, Artress and a team of people carefully measured the floor design at Chartres and then recreated it in Grace Cathedral, first painted on canvas and then woven into a huge floor tapestry. Thousands of women and men regularly visit the cathedral to walk the labyrinth. It's been so successful that an outdoor terrazzo version has been created on the cathedral's plaza for use when the building is closed. More than a thousand labyrinths are now in use in churches of many denominations as people recover their connection with the sacred, all because one woman, Lauren Artress, found a compelling way to nurture others.

Nurturing Men

The inability of congregations to nurture men is particularly troublesome and difficult. Since 1990, studies have repeatedly shown that American men—almost 90 percent of whom profess a belief in God or a higher power—are increasingly unchurched. Men's worship attendance, Bible reading, financial support, and volunteering have all steadily declined in many mainstream congregations. There are exceptions, of course, but in general men don't feel that the

Church has much to offer them. Woody Davis, writing in *Net Results* (June 2001), researched why men are not attracted to the Church, yet are attracted to other volunteer organizations. Men are not less religious, he found, it's that they don't identify with current imagery and themes which they see as essentially gender inappropriate. What can be done? Here are a few possibilities, and a specific example, of how to assist men in their spiritual journey.

Make the Good News Relevant

Feelings of disconnection and loneliness are spiritual issues of real importance, though most men don't want to discuss them in detail. If they could connect and be with other men in a nonthreatening setting where they could build relationships, authentic nurture would be encouraged. Men's ministry thrives best in a relaxed, low-key, nonthreatening environment. However, men do express a desire for coherent and systematic explanation of the relevance of the Christian message in their lives, and in the lives of their community and beyond.

Provide Practical Solutions to Life's Challenges

Creative ministries based on the real needs that men express, not simply preconceptions the congregation may have about what they think men need, stress practical solutions based upon spiritual principles to contemporary challenges. Thus how-to ministry can be a powerful way to nurture the spiritual growth of men. A congregation that is serious about bringing more men into a relationship with God should be open to innovative ways to attract men:

- A concert rather than a worship service
- A social event
- A service project, especially one that serves the larger community
- A seminar or workshop on a theme currently popular with men

Men who are parents want the best for their kids, which includes appropriate moral education and values clarification. Even if they had mediocre or negative experiences in church when they were children and may be skeptical of the ability of the congregation to do this, they hope that this special education can be accomplished through quality children's worship and programming.

Wisdom Ways Resource Center for Spirituality in St. Paul, Minnesota, is a good example of how the tactics we have mentioned can be woven into a men's spirituality series. One of their offerings is Storytelling and Soul-Making. Among the areas of discussion are Men and God: Finding Our Focus, Men and Sports: Finding Our Passion, and Men and Family: Finding Our Vision. These meetings are open to men of all religious backgrounds. They are intended as an opportunity for men, in a relaxed setting of discussion and good food, to explore spiritual topics that are relevant to them.

Spiritual Explorers: Getting Acquainted with Your Community of Faith

At some point, a newcomer will consider formal membership. All too often, he or she is invited into membership without understanding the serious commitment to be made. Generally, congregations seem to believe that if they make membership an easy and painless process, their rolls will be filled with supportive new people eager to grow in the faith. But this hasn't happened. There is a lesson to be learned in what far-thinking progressive congregations realized years ago: the welcoming process should be made as easy as possible, but membership as challenging as possible. Congregations often do the reverse, making welcoming difficult and complex and membership easy. If the newcomer has been nurtured to the point where membership is the next step in growth, it is all the more important that the individual clearly grasp the commitment being made. We feel this is best done through a required process.

The Spiritual Explorers Class is a process of exploration for those who want to learn more about the practice of the spiritual life through a congregation. Many newcomers find it a challenge to meet people, make friends, and find ways to be involved in the life of a congregation. Through this class, participants have an opportunity to meet others, make friends in a small group, and be given tools and information that help them become acquainted with the life and ministry of the congregation. The class is offered for exploratory purposes, so there is no obligation to join at its conclusion (though many do). In addition, current members should be invited to refresh their knowledge of the congregation, its history, its teachings, and their own ministry within the community of faith.

Typically, the Explorers Class meets quarterly, or twice yearly. We use a seven-week format, but if a shorter time is seen as beneficial the class can be tailored to meet time requirements. Each class meets weekly for two hours. During the first hour, a staff member gives a lecture and a PowerPoint presentation or slide show, on a specific aspect of the life and work of the church. A short break follows. During the second hour, participants meet in small groups with a trained facilitator, where they have the opportunity to share their own story of faith and get to know others on the spiritual journey. A suggested format is given in Exhibit 4.2.

Strengthening Your Nurturing System

The Spiritual Explorers Class is a particularly effective tactic that strengthens the entire nurturing system. Here are a few others that have worked well in a variety of congregational settings.

"Getting to Know Us" Orientation Coffee

A good welcoming and nurturing activity to introduce people to the community of faith is a regularly scheduled coffee orientation, for example on the first Sunday of the month. This activity brings selected members and people interested in learning more about your congregation together for a time of sharing and exploring and for an opportunity to meet others. The senior pastor, a staff member,

Exhibit 4.2. Suggested Curriculum for the Spiritual Explorers Class

WEEK ONE
Values, Mission, Vision, World View, and How the
Congregation Shares the Good News
Lecture or presentation topic: "The 'Gospel' According to
_____ Church"
   Small-group theme: getting to know each other—our past

- With whom did you live between the ages of seven and eleven?
  Where did you live?
- How was that home heated? To whom did you go for warmth during
  those years?
- When did you first experience God's love? (An individual may have
  never had this experience; that's OK, and it can be part of the sharing.)

WEEK TWO
A Focus on Denominational History and Traditions as
Reflected Through this Congregation
Lecture or presentation topic: "An Overview of Our Denominational
History"
   Small-group theme: getting to know each other—our present

- Describe your current "work" situation. What is most satisfying? most
  frustrating? most challenging?
- Describe an important relationship you are in now. What do you
  experience as most satisfying in it? most frustrating? most challenging?

WEEK THREE
Introduction to the Spiritual Life, and Various Methods of Prayer
Lecture or presentation topic: "The Importance of Prayer for Effective
Daily Living"
   Small-group theme: looking to the future

- What is your most important unfulfilled dream? What can you do
  about it?
- Do you have a personal need or concern you'd like us to pray for
  during the week?

(Continued)

Exhibit 4.2. Continued

Spiritual Autobiographies
Beginning with the next meeting, we'll begin reading "spiritual autobiographies." Each person is encouraged to participate.

Outline for Your Spiritual Autobiography
1. Your autobiography should be one single-spaced word-processed page or two handwritten pages, or if you feel creative you could do a brief audio or video presentation.
2. You will be asked to read your paper aloud to the group.
3. This is a recollection of key events and people who have most influenced you and your values on your spiritual journey. The focus is *now*, where you are at this time.
4. Please don't wait to write this at the last minute. Begin after this session to collect your thoughts about yourself. Work on it each day.
5. We suggest that you specifically write about these four questions:
   What have I experienced so far on my spiritual journey, and who are the key people who have influenced my values and my thinking?
   Where am I now (or am I not) on my spiritual journey?
   What am I looking for on my spiritual journey?
   Where do I think God is touching my life right now? (or) Where do I wish God would touch my life right now?

WEEK FOUR
Opportunities to Grow Through Classes, Groups, and Workshops
Lecture or presentation topic: "The Life and Work of ___ Church"
   Small-group session: read and discuss individual spiritual autobiographies.

WEEK FIVE
Getting Involved: Volunteer Opportunities
Lecture or presentation topic: "How You Can Get Involved in Our Church" (People in charge of volunteer activities are invited to give a brief pitch for their particular opportunity.)
   Small-group session: read and discuss spiritual autobiographies

WEEK SIX
Giving as a Way to Grow Spiritually
Lecture or presentation topic: "Tithing (or Giving) Means More Than Money"
  Small-group session: personal sharing

- What has participating in this class meant to you?
- Option: exchange small and inexpensive gifts as tokens of friendship. These might include homemade or handmade items, cards, bookmarks, and so on. There are two possibilities: participants and facilitators provide gifts for each member, or each person draws one name by lot.

WEEK SEVEN
Taking the Next Step
All participants meet to learn the next steps in growing together in faith.
  Theme: growing together in faith

1. The senior pastor addresses the group on the subject of commitment.
2. Participants engage in a time of silence, a guided meditation, or a short worship service.
3. A survey of spiritual gifts is completed by each person to find his or her particular form of ministry in the congregation.
4. The date and time of the Sunday service to receive new members is discussed. Are there any particular requirements for that day? Is there a rehearsal? Who is invited? What shall participants wear?
5. Those being admitted to the congregation personalize and address invitations to family and friends for the Sunday service.

---

or a lay-leader briefly reviews the spiritual DNA of the congregation and responds to questions. This orientation provides:

- A forum for introducing discipleship
- Fellowship between existing members and new people
- A way to disseminate information about the activities of the congregation
- An introduction to lay-leaders and professional staff

Sponsors, Mentors, Friends

The sponsor, mentor, or friend might take responsibility for any of several nurturing activities in relation to individuals:

- Listen for how the congregation can be more effective in meeting their needs.

- Introduce them to others in the congregation.

- Help the individual get into a small group.

- Invite the individual to appropriate congregation sponsored events.

The tactic of sponsor, mentor, or friend should be offered as a choice for new members, so it should not be imposed.

Pastoral Care Card System

A personal letter, note, or card on a special occasion communicates to the recipient that the congregation cares for its members and friends. These might include congratulations, get well, encouragement, support, thank-you, graduation, anniversary, birthday, new baby, new home, and so on.

The late Bishop of Massachusetts, Anson Phelps Stokes, once commented humorously about the necessity of keeping these lists current. It was his practice to sign batches of cards well in advance and to rely on his staff to send out the appropriate card at the appropriate time. On one occasion, his office slipped up and sent a birthday card, much to the chagrin of the bishop, to a man who had died, and at whose funeral the bishop had recently officiated!

Telecare Ministry

Continuing telecare contact is a powerful means of keeping in touch. Each person on the congregation's mailing list should receive a periodic phone call, for any of these purposes:

- To help prevent back-door loss

- To keep up with what's going on in the person's life

- To take prayer requests

- To be effective in following up with visitors and long-term members alike

Recognition of New Members

Everyone who takes the Explorers Class and becomes a member of the congregation should be acknowledged in some form. Plan a meaningful Sunday service to receive them into the fellowship of the congregation. This service should include these elements:

1. Introduction of the new members (done by the pastor, the lay-leader, or liturgist)
2. Affirmation of commitment by the new members to the congregation, and by the congregation to the new members
3. Appropriate ritual or ceremony receiving them into the congregation
4. A special fellowship time with good food and decorations
5. Names and photographs of the new members featured in parish newsletters and posted on bulletin boards

What to Do About Inactives

Nurturing also includes reaching out in a caring way to "inactives," those who have dropped out of the life of the congregation because they did not feel welcomed and needed; have been hurt, or perceived they have been hurt; or were unhappy or discontent over some issue or policy.

John Savage of L.E.A.D. Consultants did a study of dropouts and found congregational leaders insensitive to the "need of those persons who were aching and leaving the church." He notes that 100 percent of inactives interviewed said that no one had ever contacted them. People have told us that they wait for up to six weeks in a sort of holding pattern to see if any one will contact them, before they look around for another church home.

Keep attendance records (see discussion of the communications card in Chapter Three) to know who has not been at church for a few weeks. Call them and let them know that they are missed. Ask if there's anything the congregation can do for them right now. Let them know that you hope that they will return soon.

Hurts or Perceived Hurts

If you know the circumstances, and the congregation was neglectful, you can attempt to make amends. It may require active listening to help people over their hurt. Remind them they're always welcome. Follow up with a letter. If the hurt was a perception with no basis in fact, assist the person in seeing the accurate picture.

Unhappiness or Discontent

If people leave over an *essential* philosophical, doctrinal, or administrative difference, you might not want to seek them out, especially if the problem that caused them to leave cannot be resolved to their satisfaction if they do come back. If resolution can be achieved, welcome them back.

Nurture Is a Continuing Process

Nurture is continuing care on the spiritual journey. It is essential to provide it for new and for long-term members by:

Communicating love

Accepting them unconditionally

Responding to their felt needs

Encouraging them in their walk of faith

Newcomers who are moving toward the center of the life and work of the congregation are young organisms in the body of the church. They need nurture, care, and support to grow spiritually. The nurturing system is a process whereby growth can be encouraged. As with the other systems, this system must reflect your congregation's spiritual DNA by being understood as a way to implement the congregation's purpose as it travels in the direction of your vision.

The nurturing process is best carried out by small groups and teams, where relationships can be built. The nurturing process is strengthened by understanding that people experience God's presence in a variety of ways. No one size fits all. The nurturing activities you offer should reflect the diversity that life represents.

5

Yes, You Can
Your Empowering System

Your congregation has an untapped gold mine of creative and talented people waiting to be used in God's service. Each individual has a natural inner yearning to act unselfishly; behind this yearning is a profound motivation to experience and to express God's love.

Your congregation is a primary way to bring people to spiritual maturity. It is a place for people to gather in common worship, experience love, receive support and encouragement, and be empowered and equipped for ministry. Each of us "has been blessed with one of God's many wonderful gifts to be used in the service of others" (1 Peter 4:10).

Empowering as a system promotes growth for the congregation as a whole and for the individuals within it. A healthy empowering system invites prospective volunteers to ask the question, "What gifts, talents, or passions do I have to share?" By working with them to answer this question, the congregation creates a strong, healthy, system that can expand its ability to help people discern a ministry opportunity and then train, support, and deploy them.

Too often, a congregation sees involvement solely in a particular parochial context. It's so easy to slip into the "we need" mode: we need more Sunday school teachers, more ushers, more greeters, more people to serve on the ever-expanding number of committees and commissions. We need this, we need that. It is, of course, right and proper for the congregation to ask, "How can we get more volunteers so the work of ministry can get done?" But the individual's question, about whether God has gifted him or her with a ministry, deserves equal consideration. To do this, a congregation must be willing to present the opportunity for people to explore their own potential, assist them to discover the joys of ministry, and share with them the satisfaction to be derived from serving. Ideally the congregation is led, as Parker Palmer writes, "by people who know who they are from top to bottom, whose identity does not depend on a specific role that might be taken away at any given moment. If you are in that kind of organization, you are with people and in settings that give you identity, that empowers you to be someone."

This includes realizing that as God's children we achieve our fullest expression, individually and collectively, through unselfish caring for others. How we choose to implement that caring varies. Volunteering in the local community and through the local congregation are two important ways to express the love of God.

Volunteering Is Good for the Soul

No matter where you live, all around you are infinite ways to get involved in a life-enriching ministry. Prayer for discernment can reveal a whole universe of possibility, to help an individual feel good about accomplishing something for God, and help the beneficiaries feel good about themselves. David Owen Ritz adds this dimension: "When we give of ourselves in service, [God] will always use us to promote the growth of others in unexpected and wonderful ways; but we will always be the main beneficiary of that transaction." Volunteer ministry is a conscious expression of one's commitment to God's call.

Jesus saw the value of giving of oneself as a means of growing spiritually. He began his own ministry by responding to the needs of others—feeding them, comforting them, visiting them in their homes, praying with them, speaking to them honestly about the religious and social injustices of his time. He encouraged others to join him in what he believed God called him to do. His life is a model for ministry.

Volunteer Johnnie Plain uses Jesus as her role model. She says, "I am motivated to volunteer out of my own sense of spirituality. Jesus said that he had come to serve, not to be served. He said that when we do something for others, we do it for God. I believe that, and I act from that. For me, that means that I should consider the needs of others and how I can be of service. And I've also learned to stop thinking about what I'm giving up and to think more about what I get out of it, which is a whole lot. Why do I volunteer? It's the right thing to do."

A variety of factors encourage people to volunteer, to give of themselves:

- They have a need for personal significance. They want to feel that what they do makes a difference—in their own lives and in the lives of others.

- They volunteer when they perceive a need. They want to know that something worthwhile has resulted from their time and effort; that they are carrying out the mission of the congregation; and that they have made a valuable contribution, no matter how small it may be.

- They volunteer when they are *asked*—that is, as a result of personal contact. They appreciate the trust, confidence, and enthusiasm a congregation has for their abilities by asking them to give of themselves.

- They volunteer in response to values. If the congregation is acting on a value people perceive to be personally important, the more likely they are to be motivated to participate.

- They volunteer for specific causes, and they make a significant commitment to what they see to be a noble purpose.

If people are willing to commit to serving, then why is overall volunteering on the decline in congregations? Is it just a case of mainstream malaise, or is it symptomatic of a growing trend in society as a whole? We feel it's both.

The Problem of Malaise: Challenging the Hierarchy

Let's look first at mainstream malaise and the internal challenges of attitude and structure reflected in many congregations. The still-popular hierarchical model supposes that major decisions should be handed down by the leadership, as if from on high. This old model is resistant to organic systemic change, hampers the emergence of new leaders, stifles creativity, and makes it difficult for people to become engaged in meaningful ministry. The underlying issue is less about ministry and more about who decides who can or who can't be involved—it's us against them. There are so many disempowering layers in the decision-making process that participation becomes a zero-sum game. Unhealthy control issues can dominate the life of the congregation and have a deadening effect on ministry initiatives. Volunteers serving under this mind-set often view it as a burdensome duty motivated by institutional needs and driven by guilt. The result: no ministry of significance happens.

A pastor recently shared this story with us. Mary Riley, one of his parishioners, is a professional with a young child. She came to him with a wonderful idea for bringing together other professional women to learn more about the Bible, and through that study share insights into their lives as mothers and professionals in the workplace. She had strong support from eight other women, so it was an idea ready to happen. She envisioned a weekly "prayer breakfast" with child care, where women could dig deep into scripture and explore how the Bible had relevance in their busy lives. The pastor was delighted with the idea, especially as it came from a relatively new member of the congregation. He invited her to go through the proper channels, so she met with the church board. They listened with polite interest but felt they had enough to handle that month, so they tabled further discussion to their next meeting.

A month later, the board determined that the education committee might want to review the idea and referred Mary to them. So the following month, Mary took her idea to the education committee, who felt that this was really something that the evangelism committee should handle—and they met quarterly. Mary dutifully went before the evangelism committee, who thought the idea was worthy of further study and assigned it to a subcommittee. Six months passed, the other women were beginning to lose interest, and Mary Riley began to see that she was wasting her time trying to get approvals from an archaic system. She eventually shelved her idea. On reflection, she decided that any future involvement she might have in the ministry of the parish, under the present system, was futile. Bureaucracy triumphed.

There are formidable challenges involved in changing a congregation's culture, such as reversing the top-down hierarchical model and giving people the space to decide for themselves about ministry possibilities, but these will be trumped by the enormous benefits that accrue to a congregation that uses a permission-giving empowering system. The basic idea behind it is as old as the sixteenth-century Protestant Reformation. It is anchored in the concept of the "priesthood of all believers" (1 Peter 2:5,9), that we are all—lay and ordained, women and men—called to ministry; that the laity is called into the *ministry* of the congregation, not just to the *business* of the congregation. Unfortunately, too many congregations give lip service to this doctrine and then promptly ignore it as too risky. From a hierarchical standpoint, it is not just risky; it's downright subversive because it could loosen the constricting bonds of controlling leaders. Yet precisely because it is open to risk, the idea is so powerful.

In *Church Leadership*, Lovett Weams Jr. ties ministry right back to the spiritual DNA: "Leadership can never be understood apart from mission and vision. . . . Leadership exists to make possible a preferred future for the people involved, which reflects the heart of the mission and the values to which they are committed." Leaders and laypeople should work together as a strategic team, not as antagonists. Some act as if—to paraphrase a popular book title— professionals are from Mars and volunteers are from Venus (or worse still are second-class citizens). But an astute observer on the church scene has commented that Noah's Ark, which survived the Flood, was constructed by amateurs, while the unsinkable White Star liner *Titanic* was built by pros!

To grow, a congregation must have access to a large and enthusiastic volunteer force of amateurs so the work of ministry can be accomplished. However, fewer and fewer people are willing to commit, and we are hearing reports that the 80-20 rule (80 percent of the work of the congregation being done by 20 percent of the members) is now inching closer to 90-10. This is especially so in aging congregations where the Silent and GI Generations are in charge. Having done their fair share, they are anxious to pass the torch to younger generations. Or are they?

We recall a congregation where the old guard—in this case, the Martha Guild—had been in control of women's activities for decades. Their big annual event was always an elegant dinner during which the invited women were encouraged to join the guild. For many years, this was effective, but as time passed and fewer new women joined the group, their ranks gradually diminished. Clearly, it was time to hand the annual dinner over to younger women, who they assumed would be younger versions of themselves. So a new group got together and happily agreed to host the annual dinner.

Now, this was a labor of love. Many of them had full-time jobs, and some of the married women not only worked but had families to care for. On the night of the dinner, the old guard formed a delegation to "inspect" the work, and dropped in an hour or so before the scheduled time. The younger women, justly proud of their efforts, welcomed them effusively. The menu was elegant, the tables were beautifully laid, the decorations and floral arrangements were exquisite.

The old guard silently walked around checking out the arrange-ments. Finally, one of them said, with nods of agreement from her associates, "No, no, no, you haven't got it right. It's all wrong."

The young women, who had given up so much of their time and worked so hard to create a pleasant evening, were stunned by the comment. "What haven't we got right? What's wrong?" one of them asked. "We've worked hard to make this a success." They were sternly advised that the napkins had always been under the silver-ware, not folded fancily and placed on the plates. "Well, you'll have to change this," they were told, "it isn't the way we do it here." The younger women looked at each other in amazement, but they said nothing and quietly rearranged the napkins. The dinner went off without a hitch and received glowing reviews. But not a single word of congratulations did they receive from the old guard. Several weeks later, the younger women met and formed their own group.

At another parish across town, the folks there would answer yes, they are quite willing to empower others, and they did it—though it was a very challenging and eye-opening process. The older leader-ship had realized for several years that it was time to let the younger generations take over. They talked and talked and talked about it. They met and met and met over it. Some of the longtime leaders argued that a significant vetting period was essential. How long? They weren't sure. But it had to be a lengthy one, or how else would the younger folks learn? Others wondered exactly what, if any, skills and talents the younger folks had to contribute to the congregation. Would they continue the tried and true ways, or would they want to change things?

Finally, one sage, who had sat quietly listening all those past months, rapped on the table to get their attention. Standing up, he said, "Friends, listen to me for just a minute. Have you forgotten that most of the questions you are asking about them were asked about us some thirty years ago? Didn't they give us our chance? Shouldn't we give them theirs?" They all remembered and were suitably chastened—or at least most of them were. Ultimately, their decision was to trust God and to turn the care and nurture of the congregation over to a completely new cadre of leaders.

The Problem of Privatization: I'd Rather Do It Myself!

The second major challenge to greater participation in communities of faith is the pervasive *privatization* of society. This is an emerging social challenge, not of the Church's making but nonetheless affecting the Church. Greta Garbo's famous line "I want to be alone" is becoming a reality, as Robert Putnam argues in *Bowling Alone: The Collapse and Revival of American Community*. He says that social isolation and declining community engagement is a serious concern for all aspects of contemporary American society. Involvement has lessened—all the way from the PTA to the historic fraternal lodges, from political parties to labor unions, from the scouts to bowling leagues. Yet some organizations have actually expanded their bases: notably, the Sierra Club, Greenpeace, and the American Association of Retired Persons. Why have they increased numerically while others have declined?

Part of the answer is found in the increasing privatization of social connections. One can easily and effortlessly support these organizations through reading newsletters and responding to financial appeals simply by writing checks. This passive involvement does not require one's presence with others in authentic community. Symptoms of this increasing privatization can be seen in the insularity that is inherent in our computer culture. It's easy to point, click, and purchase a large array of goods and services online, including full meals, groceries, airplane tickets, and even automobiles. It's called "convenience," and to an extent it is, but at what price? In the cyber world, conversations do take place, and electronic relationships are built, but they are between individuals who typically never meet face to face. This minimizes valuable personal interaction and can lead to isolation, so it's no surprise that loneliness, in this age of the communications superhighway, has become a significant spiritual issue.

Putnam further points out that although America has more church buildings per capita than any other nation, religious sentiment seems to be less tied to religious institutions and is becoming more self-defined, as expressed in the number of individuals who are exploring alternative spiritualities on their own, thus making community more difficult. Community is a foundational concept of the Church. Christianity is, after all, a community-centered religion, not simply a point of view or a philosophy to study. Jesus said, "I have come that you might have life," and life must be actively, consciously, and regularly experienced in relationship with others. Privatization of faith makes this kind of community less likely. But God moves in mysterious ways, and it may work out that the effects of privatization on the Church will serve as a wake-up call.

In *The Once and Future Church*, Loren Mead addresses the dilemma congregations now face in this time of transition: "The shells of the old structures still surround us even though many of them no longer work. Some of the structures are institutions, some are roles, some are mind-sets and expectations. At one moment they mediate grace to us and at the next they block and confuse us. Sometimes some of them actually support and nourish us, while others get in the way of the new structures we need. *Our task is no less than the reinvention of the church.* It may take several generations. We will not see the end of it, but we must begin now." (italics in the original)

Congregations want easy answers and quick fixes, preferably within the safety of their present structure and with a minimum of change and disruption. Unfortunately, there are no easy answers and no quick fixes. There is, though, opportunity for emerging new forms of ministry that deserve attention.

Permission-Giving: Actualizing the Empowering System

Most people are unaccustomed to thinking of themselves as "ministers." In general, they consider the term to belong exclusively to the ordained clergy. Think again. Your congregation has an incredible opportunity to give impetus to the renewal of lay ministry. You create new avenues for spiritual growth, and you upgrade volunteering to a new level of ministry by providing ways for people to creatively live out your mission. The Gallup Organization found that 40 percent of all congregational members have expressed interest in having a ministry—but they've never been asked. You need to educate people to understand that they do, indeed, have the capacity for ministry; to help them discover where God is calling them to serve; to assist them in working out what they're good at— what they're most interested in doing—and how they want to contribute their time. When rightly employed to carry out your mission, the empowering system can help people fit in better and give dignity and joy to each member in service to their community of faith. As individuals grow spiritually, your congregation grows.

Permission-giving makes it possible and desirable for one to discover one's gifts, talents, and passions, and explore how they can be used for ministry. Permission-giving is creating an environment in which control is less important than creativity. It recognizes that life is about change. It celebrates willingness to embrace change. It is an understanding that life is self-organizing and self-replicating. Rather than struggle against these realities, permission-giving is a decision by the congregation to "let go and let God" express through them. This includes understanding that things may not always be done right, but that the right things will be done in an atmosphere of relaxed openness.

A permission-giving environment encourages individuals to look at each ministry opportunity as a unique way to serve others by "building up the church, the body of Christ, to a position of strength and maturity" (Ephesians 4:12, TLB). Imagine the level of inner peace, satisfaction, and sense of ownership that can be realized by being part of a community where people, as the hymn says, "give to the Lord the best of their service." This is a place where the doctrine of the priesthood of all believers is taken seriously.

At first glance, the term *permission-giving* might seem to imply an everything-goes, freewheeling, no-holds-barred approach. Just the opposite is the case. Permission-giving is based on clear understanding of your spiritual DNA—your core values, mission, and vision, as well as those inherited aspects of identity that are truly important. It means allowing people to carry out ministry in accordance with that DNA. Everything is measured according to it; what doesn't fit isn't done. Ministries that have been in place but no longer fit are allowed to gently fade away. A permission-giving congregation is so clear about its purpose that it trusts people to determine for themselves how to fulfill that purpose. Such a congregation is committed to seeing in people what God sees in them, and to helping them discover and use it. There is no particular form for permission-giving; the forms vary depending on local circumstances, denomination, and congregational culture.

Some see this type of environment as too chaotic, others as too passive. The fear is of either ministry without accountability or no ministry at all. Our experience has shown that neither view fully grasps the infinite possibilities for ministry based on faith rather than on fear, on empowering rather than on control. Permission-giving is a new way to support and encourage using the leadership gifts of lay people; therefore a congregation has to be open to this approach. It can't function alongside the old model. Permission-giving is messy and may seem confusing, but so is the world in which we live. This approach requires faith, trust, and mutual respect to work. Permission-giving emphasizes accountability, not control; but it also stresses accountability to the congregation's spiritual identity. Bill Easum's book *Sacred Cows Make Gourmet Burgers* says a permission-giving congregation believes "that the role of God's people is to minister to people in the world, every day of the week," who "encourage on-the-spot decision making," and whose leaders are "secure enough to equip others for ministry and then get out of the way."

Opportunities Flow Naturally

There are, of course, distinct boundaries in the permission-giving model. They are found in your congregation's spiritual DNA.

Within those boundaries, all ministries for which you have passion, gifts, and resources are permitted.

Instead of the leaders prescribing specific activities that should, or may, or may not, be done, all activities are permitted, indeed encouraged, as long as they are not proscribed by the boundaries. No one individual can stop ministry from going forward, because it is the spiritual DNA that determines whether or not a ministry is within the boundaries. Those who say no to a new idea must present their reasons, founded on the same criteria. Catholic philosopher Anthony De Mello has an interesting analogy in his book *Awakening: The Perils and Opportunities of Reality*: "And look at the river as it moves toward the sea. It creates its own banks that contain it. When there's something within you that moves in the right direction, it creates its own discipline." In a permission-giving atmosphere, opportunities for service flow naturally within the banks created by the congregation's spiritual DNA. This creates a sense of ownership unimagined by the top-down model.

King of Kings Lutheran Church in Shelby Township, Michigan, went through a process of articulating its mission and restructuring for permission-giving ministry. Pastor Louis Forney describes the process:

> Since God is in charge, we decided to let people carry out the work God has given us. The mission of the congregation became the direction of our ministry. *We stopped discussing everything, everywhere, and just did ministry. Since that time, self-starting and self-directing ministry teams have grown up everywhere.* They are encouraged to see and meet needs. If something is consistent with our mission, it happens. No one stops ministry from moving forward! Responsibility for ministry rests in the hands of the people of God—where it belongs. In some ways, the church has turned upside-down. Leaders teach people the mission and equip them to do ministry. We give people what they need to do, what they are here to do. As

> we trust and empower people, our ministry has exploded.
> It has been a long journey, but now we have over 90 per-
> cent of our members actively serving in over 100 min-
> istries. *We are now mission focused and permission-giving.*
> *It works!* (italics in original)

We see, from Forney's quote, that ministry was freed up to
develop naturally rather than attempting to manage it. The leaders
understood that everyone is a potential leader on the basis of their
spiritual giftedness. This congregation happened to be ready for a
new model. It took a while, but eventually the results spoke for
themselves—self-starting, self-directing teams have arisen naturally
from within the congregation. In *Leadership and the New Science,*
Margaret Wheatley writes that the quantum world "teaches that
there are no pre-fixed, definitely describable destinations. There are
instead potentials that will form into real ideas. . . ." This tells us
that if we trust God to unfold through us, there are limitless ways
people can serve. It suggests that life is fundamentally self-organizing and that the congregation's most effective and harmonious role
is not control but empowerment.

Permission-Giving in Action

So long as something is not proscribed by the genetic boundaries
established by a congregation's DNA, worship teams should be given
the freedom to be creative in finding powerful pathways to God.

Children's Worship

Two examples focus on children, not as the hope of the future but
as important constituents right now. The Church of the Redeemer
of San Rafael, California, offered Sunday School as a traditional
means of reaching children, though only a few showed up each
week. Billie Barbash, director of children's education, working with
Pastor Jeremy Blodgett and a worship team, began to see children's
ministry in a different light. From that, they were willing to risk

abolishing the old model in favor of a newly created worship experience called Kids' Church, targeted for younger Millennials.

Similarly, when St. Paul's Church, in the same city, decided on an innovative worship experience for children, Associate Rector Lynn Oldham-Robinett, encouraged by Rector Bruce Bramlett, assembled a ministry team of people who had a strong desire to create a service focused on the spiritual needs of children, with an added dimension of empowering children as participants and as leaders. The clergy and people of the congregation felt sufficiently comfortable with their spiritual identity as a "compassionate haven" to be open and permission-giving; thus was born Where the Wild Things Worship.

Kids' Church and Wild Things are relaxed and informal short worship experiences—about forty minutes—in which the children are active participants and decision makers. As an added benefit, these services attract the kids' young parents (notably their dads), and even their proud grandparents, thus creating what many mainstream congregations have dreamed of for years: a truly intergenerational worshiping community. Only in a permission-giving environment would Kids' Church and Wild Things be possible.

Open to the Spirit

We have also witnessed how a ministry team can numerically grow and replicate in a permission-giving and supportive environment. Rob Droste, associate for church growth at Trinity Church in San Francisco, is committed to using ministry teams in a permission-giving environment. He designed a commissioning ritual for use within the regular Sunday service to underscore the fact that teams are representative of the entire congregation. During a commissioning Rob paused and addressed the congregation, asking if any felt God's call to participate in this particular ministry. After a few moments of prayerful silence, additional people came forward to commit themselves to the work of the congregation. Permission-giving, at that moment, became more than an interesting idea. What started out simply as part of a liturgical service became an encounter with God by offering people an opportunity for self-transformation and authentic service to others.

Thank You, Ross

The leaders of New Vision United Methodist Church in Millbrae, California, were having difficulty with the concepts of empowering and permission-giving. They couldn't grasp how authentic ministry could take place in an open and affirming setting—yet it was apparent to everybody that their old hierarchical model was no longer effective because fewer and fewer people were doing more and more of the congregation's work. To deal with this challenge, Pastor Linda Pickens-Jones and lay-leader John Baker asked us to facilitate an open congregational meeting to explain permission-giving and explore the process of how these new ideas could expand ministry.

Following our presentation, there was a long pause as people assimilated new information. Then Ross, a long-term parishioner, stood up and rather tentatively offered to begin a new graphics team for the congregation. As he was skilled in using PowerPoint and similar computer software programs, this was an offer of substantial merit. He shared with the group that he'd never before volunteered because he didn't feel his gifts would be of use to the congregation. It wasn't on their we-need list. Now, he understood that he could share his talent by creating a graphics and visual arts team that would bring innovation and beauty to the worship service and educational efforts, and would enliven the congregation's Web site— all through a gift he'd been given by God.

As the leaders intently listened to his passionate talk, they had visible proof and a beginning understanding of empowerment. Through Ross's initiative, empowering and permission-giving took on a new face. Within weeks, the word was out that the congregation was willing to create new ministries in alignment with people's creativity and gifts, rather than solely from the institution's needs.

The foregoing are just a few examples of how people are empowered in a permission-giving atmosphere to create new ways of doing ministry, through using their passions and gifts.

The Advantages of Permission-Giving

Permission-giving brings five clear benefits to the congregation:

1. It increases involvement, thereby ensuring a high level of satisfaction.
2. It looks at situations individually and encourages people to take risks.
3. It creates a sense of ownership; responsibility rests in the hands of the people.
4. People are willing to invest their time, efforts, and personal resources.
5. Involved people are likely to stay connected with the congregation.

When you begin to incorporate permission-giving, you find some who are self-directing, who have clarity about their ministries, and others who initially need some form of mentoring. The role of a mentor in permission-giving is to assist people in discovering an appropriate way to use their gifts and passions. Mentors offer encouragement, support, and knowledge of available resources.

Moving to permission-giving may be a slow process. It takes time for people to get used to a new model. It may take a year or so just to lay a new foundation and paint a vision for the future. However, once people accept that your congregation is serious about it, that you are willing to take risks with them and allow them to develop ministries, you'll be approached by more and more folks. As that happens, you must be ready to respond with reassurance, direction, encouragement, and trust.

Discerning Spiritual Gifts

Self-understanding is an important aspect of empowering and per-mission-giving. The early Church recognized that God gives a diversity of gifts (1 Corinthians 12–14, Romans 12, Ephesians 4, 1 Peter 4). According to scripture, we each have been given spe-cific spiritual gifts. My gift is teaching, your gift is leadership, another person's gift is administration, and so on. These are gifts of God's grace, freely given out of the unconditional love of God; like Robert Browning's "imprisoned splendor," they are just waiting to be released. Rick Isbell, minister of program at Church Street United Methodist Church in Knoxville, Tennessee, says, "No mat-ter what gifts we have, no matter where or with whom we use them, we are the body of Christ called forth to serve in his Name."

Discerning one's gifts is usually accomplished through a survey or inventory, typically in the form of a series of questions. It's a pretty straightforward process for most of the surveys: read the ques-tion, and then reply by ticking off one or more categories. The responses are tallied up and the results used as guidelines for deter-mining which gift or gifts the person possesses. As we've indicated in the previous chapter, surveys can be administered during a new-member event, or at a special volunteer ministry event, or at a parishwide ministry fair. Though churched adults are by and large cognizant of the term *spiritual gifts*, many people—even long-term members of a congregation—have no idea what their gifts are. Fewer than one out of four can identify a spiritual gift they believe they possess, so a survey can even be given to those already involved in ministry to uncover their unused or underused gifts.

Contemporary spiritual gifts originated in an 1976 article in *Eternity* magazine by Richard Houts, of the North American Bap-tist Seminary, himself author of the "Houts Inventory of Spiritual Gifts." Most religious supply houses carry a variety of surveys, and there are even surveys that can be taken, and scored, on the Inter-net. Some are long, some are short. Houts's survey has 128 questions. The "Trenton Spiritual Gifts Analysis" has 85 questions. There's a shorter "Spiritual Gifts Survey" of 45 questions by Calvie Hughson Schwalm, published by Crystal Cathedral. For a contemporary approach, see *LifeKeys: Discovering Who You Are, Why You're Here and What You Do Best,* by David Stark, Sandra Hirsch, and Jane Kise. Larry Gilbert has written a child-friendly booklet with scripture passages on spiritual gifts, titled *God's Special Gift for Me.* Jane Kise and Kevin Johnson have written *Find Your Fit: Dare to Act on God's Gift for You,* an approach to talents and gifts for teenagers.

The survey you choose should reflect the personality of your congregation. The primary intent is to get people involved in active ministry on the basis of their passions, gifts, and talents and, of course, their desire to serve.

Let Me Use My Gift My Way

Betty Hollister of Terra Linda's Lutheran Church of the Resurrection tangibly manifests her gifts each Christmas Eve. Betty can't participate as actively in the life of the congregation as she once did, but she still wants to do her part. She uses her artistic gifts for God, each year by handcrafting Christmas decorations. Betty and Pastor Lon Haack decide what the year's theme is, and she creates three-dimensional decorations in keeping with that theme. In the past she has created angels, wise men, and candle designs. She buys her own materials and spends months working on the project. These decorations are extremely well made, with up to six hours of handwork going into each of the one hundred decorations. On Christmas Eve, these beautiful creations appear under the large sanctuary Christmas tree, from which they are distributed to the children. Few people know who has provided them. Betty wants it that way; she doesn't expect any glory from it. "Payment" comes from the happy children who each year look forward to a new creation.

A few years ago, the Roper Organization found that young working Americans now have sixteen hours less discretionary time each week than their counterparts had in the 1970s. With less time to offer, your congregation should ensure that people's time is used wisely. Whenever you dissipate a volunteer's hours on committees; in meetings; or working on budgets, elections, and other organizational procedures, you waste an important asset. Most maintenance activities can be done by staff, which would free up volunteer hours for meaningful ministry.

Julie Smith is a good example. She heard a stirring sermon by her pastor and was fired up to serve her congregation. She's a teacher at the local high school. The congregation desperately needed volunteer teachers, especially working with high school youth. Here's how the leaders sized up the situation: "We need teachers. She's a teacher. She gets the job." The leaders took it for granted that Julie would want to use her free time doing what she does many hours each day. "Let's put Ms. Smith in charge of the new youth group," they decided; "she'll be perfect for that job."

Of course she was, from their standpoint, the right person for the job. However, they considered only the institution's immediate needs and completely overlooked asking Julie what she'd like to do, or helping her discern her other gifts. In fact, Julie did not want to teach; she was interested in exploring some other facet of her personality that had little or nothing to do with her occupation. The leaders at first were miffed with her and nearly refused to let her volunteer at all. Julie persisted. She wanted to fulfill her passion: working with senior adults. She's doing it now, and she's doing a fantastic job.

On the other hand, as Mary Schramm points out in her insightful book *Gifts of Grace*, "if using our gifts and sensing fulfillment and peace is associated with our work week, we can thank God." This reminds us that there are folks who don't get to use their professional skills imaginatively and creatively on the job but would find it completely appropriate and satisfying to use and expand them for their community of faith.

The bottom line here is never to assume. Always ask.

The Interview Process

An important way to assist someone in discerning a volunteer role is to schedule an interview. The primary purpose of the interview is to get acquainted with the individual by understanding his or her needs ("How can we serve you, and what can we do to help you grow in your faith?"). The interview is also about discerning the gifts and passions of the individual ("How can we help you feel fulfilled and find you a place of meaningful service?").

The job of the interviewer is to *listen*, not to slot the individual into a predetermined spot. It is a discerning process, in which sufficient time is allowed for listening as well as speaking. Prospective volunteers take a spiritual gifts survey, and then a one-on-one interview is scheduled by the volunteer coordinator or a team member. Because the interview is an open-ended process, we suggest a few basic guidelines:

- Establish an agreed-upon time frame for the interview in advance.

- It takes place in a room or locale where there are no interruptions.

- The interview begins and ends with prayer.

- The spiritual DNA of the congregation is reviewed.

- The results of the spiritual gifts survey can serve as a basis for the discussion.

- If there is an existing opportunity that suits the person's gifts, she or he should be invited to explore it (for four to six weeks) to see if there is a good fit. A notebook of current ministry job descriptions should be available.

Suggested Questions for the Interviewer

These questions are structured enough to give direction but open enough to permit creative speculation.

- Tell me a little about yourself. How did you come to this congregation? What brought you to this point on your spiritual journey?

- What are your hopes and dreams for yourself?

- Tell me about a high point in your life, when you were involved in something meaningful and significant to you.

- What are your hopes and dreams for our congregation? What do you feel our congregation can offer to the surrounding community?

- Your spiritual gifts survey revealed that you have the gift of _____. How might you use this gift in God's service? What would that look like?

Outline for Creating a New Ministry Activity

In the interview process, it may become apparent that the potential new volunteer would like to initiate some ministry activity that does not currently exist. In this circumstance, we recommend that you share with the person a procedure for creating a new ministry activity.

Write the Proposal

The person proposing the ministry opportunity submits a short written proposal to the appropriate team or committee. It should include:

- The purpose of the ministry and for whom it is intended (the target audience)

- How it aligns with the congregation's values, mission, and vision

- What benefits the congregation will derive from the proposed ministry

- How it will be implemented and by whom

- What resources will be required, and an estimate of the costs involved

- What the anticipated time frame is for this ministry

Evaluate the Proposal

If the proposal is in harmony with the DNA of the congregation, an interview with the person is arranged to clarify points and establish accountability (as determined by the congregation) for the project.

Empower the Project Leader

Once the proposal is approved, the person is empowered to proceed. Approval might be by letter, by recognition at a Sunday service, or at a celebration of ministries. The approval process should be short and quick, and the person should be notified as quickly as possible.

Monitor the Project

Once the ministry activity is under way, it should be monitored periodically (the congregation determines how frequently) to track progress, oversee costs, and ensure proper accountability to the DNA.

So the Body Will Grow Strong

The empowering system operates best in a culture where the congregation is aware of its strengths and weaknesses. We use the Empowering Quotient (EQ) survey for this evaluation as a quick way to scan the current health of the system (see Chapter Seven). After this scanning has been completed, the congregation considers which additional empowering tactics can be mapped to strengthen the system—tactics that the congregation tests and monitors over a period of time (say six months to a year). How do you know if the system is made stronger? The most obvious result is more people in volunteer ministry.

In this chapter, we've seen that empowering is a vital system in the body of Christ. The early Church empowered people for service, and the Church of today continues the process. Empowering others is what congregational leadership is all about. It won't be easy for some to give up long-held power and place trust in others. It won't be easy for those being empowered, either, because taking on responsibility is risky and people are often fearful about not succeeding. Yet empowering can't happen without risk. Paul writes, in Ephesians 4:11–12, that the chief reason leaders exist is to empower people, not to control them: "Christ chose some of us to be [servant-leaders] so that his people would learn to serve and his body would grow strong." This is the heart of the empowering system.

6

How May We Help You?
Your Serving System

There's an old parable about a farmer who had lived a long and fruitful life. He was a pillar of the community, always ready to be there for others, always ready to give a helping hand, never saying no to a reasonable request, and willing to go the extra mile. In the course of his life, the old farmer derived enormous spiritual strength from serving. But his time had come to enter the kingdom, so God sent an angel to him. "I can't go right now," he said to the startled angel. "Some of my neighbors rely on me. The harvest was late this year, and the Smiths need help gathering their crops. Please tell God that I am not being ungrateful; can I postpone entering the kingdom just for a while?" So the angel departed.

Several years later, the angel came back and reminded him that it was time. "It's not possible for me to go now," the farmer said. "We had a flood here and I'm needed to help folks rebuild their homes, or they'll freeze during the winter. Please explain to God that I must stay here, at least for a while longer." The angel departed.

Every year thereafter the angel returned, and every year, on the basis of his latest explanation, the man asked for and got a deferment.

Finally, extreme old age caught up with him, he'd done all he could do, and he was ready for the angel to come for him. He prayed, "God, I suppose you think I'm ungrateful, and maybe you got the impression that I don't want to be with you. I do. It's just that there was always so much to do. So, God, please send your angel back; I'm ready."

The angel instantly appeared. "I'm ready to enter the kingdom of God forever," the old man said to the angel.

The angel burst into laughter. "Where do you think you've been all these years?"

This parable is a reminder that in serving others we are doing the work of the kingdom. We are already home when we live into Jesus' ideal, "Whenever you do something for any of my people, no matter how unimportant it may seem, you do it for me" (Matthew 25:40). This parable speaks to our time, for people today have a deep yearning for meaning and direction in their lives, and that yearning can be addressed through serving others.

Service is about growth, not about maintaining the status quo. Consider for a moment the *Antherae hartii* moth. It is a voracious eater in the larva state; but when it transforms into an adult moth it's devoid of a mouth and a digestive system. It's called the moth with no mouth; because it has no way to take in food, it starves in a few hours. It lays its eggs, and then it dies. It has developed into a function.

People are not coming to your congregation to be functions. They come because they have a deep inner desire to grow spiritually and to have a sense that they are sharing in something significant. Working with others who are also looking for meaning and direction transforms individuals, and it transforms service in the congregation from drudgery to creativity, from possibility to passion. This is what we call the serving system.

In this system, as with the other key systems, the individual and the congregation have questions that require answers. The individual asks, "How can I best use the spiritual gifts and passions God has given me?" The congregation asks, "How can we provide support and recognition for individuals who grow through serving others?" Both questions assume that there is enormous power in purposeful use of one's gift, talent, or passion.

The effects of serving have long been recognized by psychologists, clergy, and counselors, who work with people trying to get through their own personal triumphs and tragedies. They often advise these folks to get involved in a support group or growth group, where they can hear people's stories and learn about the needs of others. They hear about each other's struggles and tell of their own. Often they are touched by life stories and struggles they have not had to face. This is the type of caring and desire to share of oneself that leaders exercise in their efforts to make a difference in individuals' lives and in the life of their faith community.

The Jesus Model: "I Have Set the Example for You"

Jesus is the ideal model. Laurie Beth Jones, author of *Jesus, CEO*, writes: "The principle of service is what separates true leaders from glory seekers. Jesus, the leader, served his people. Most religions teach that we are put here to serve God; yet in Jesus, God is offering to serve us. True service inspires service. The true attitude of serving is a softening agent that works on the hardest of hearts and situations."

True leadership, then, is sharing of oneself. It means giving of one's time, talent, and energy in helping people to a better life. It's not about recognition or payment, though the personal rewards of joy and satisfaction can be tremendous. It's an act of total unselfishness.

This is not the old model, where leadership came from the top down and leaders decided what needed to be done and expected others to do the work. The model we're discussing in this chapter is leadership that demands that a leader share of himself or herself.

In John, 13:1–16, Jesus teaches by example. It was at the Passover feast, and during the meal Jesus suddenly got up, removed his outer garment, and wrapped a towel around his waist. Then he poured water into a large bowl and startled his disciples by going to each of them, washing their feet and drying them with the towel. Peter didn't like this at all. "You'll never wash my feet," he said. Jesus replied, "If I don't wash you, you don't really belong to me."

After he had finished this unusual procedure, Jesus said to them all, "Do you understand what I have done?" He reminded them that they called him "Teacher" and "Master." He said, if he as teacher and master was willing to wash their feet, they should be willing to do the same for others. "I have set the example," he told them, "and you should do for each other exactly what I have done for you." This kind of leadership moves from servitude to servanthood. Through his simple act, Jesus provided a quantum leap in understanding how we grow spiritually.

The Servant-Leader Model

In our modern world, this is called *servant-leadership*. Although it's a concept as old as the Church, it has been given new meaning as a result of a single man, Robert K. Greenleaf.

"The difference," Greenleaf writes, "manifests itself in the care taken by the servant—first to make sure that other people's highest priority needs are being served. The best test, and one difficult to administer, is: do those served grow as persons; do they, while being served, become healthier, wiser, freer, more autonomous, more likely themselves to become servants?" The scriptures provided Greenleaf ample illustrations from the ministry of Jesus. He also saw the power of servant-leadership in action in the lives of people of his century who personified servant-leadership: Mahatma Gandhi, Dietrich Bonhoeffer, Cesar Chavez, and Mother Teresa. Their lives, as with the life of Jesus, reflected the ability to serve God and respond to God's will through compassionately serving others.

A Shift from Power-Based to Mission-Centered

A servant-leader, then, is committed not to power but to mission. In a congregation's ministry teams and other small groups, success depends directly on whether the leaders embody the essential characteristics of servant-leadership. It's been our experience in working with hundreds of congregations that there is a commonality about those who lead by serving, as compared to those who simply impose their authority on others. Time and again, we've seen certain characteristics displayed in men and women who are true servant-leaders:

- Servant-leaders discern a *sense of calling* to serve God through serving others, which they do out of gratitude and as a way to grow spiritually.

- They have confidence that God will provide the strength and the resources to advance toward the vision of a desired future.

- They have a sense of awareness that serving is at the core of transformation.

- They are visionary leaders who possess a pastoral heart.

- Servant-leaders *lead from within,* displaying humility, harmony, and a sense of peace.

- They are good listeners and learners.

- They are open to change and willing to take risks.

- Servant-leaders understand, support, and embody the spiritual DNA of the congregation.

- They have the ability to build community on the basis of serving God and others.

- Servant-leaders empower others to serve through teams and small groups.

Needless to say, individuals who possess these characteristics are powerful leaders and can have a great influence on others.

Moving from *I* to *We*

Servant-leadership is an individual act. A single person can experience personal transformation in this form of ministry. However, the Church is community-based. It is where individual servant-leaders come together to create an enormous reservoir of power and use it to bring about radical change. Jesus emphasized this in Matthew 18:19–20 when he said to his followers: "I promise that when any two of you on earth agree about something you are praying for, my Father in heaven will do it for you. Whenever two or more of you come together in my name, I am there with you."

He's talking about power, the life-giving power that can be generated when people act together, with each other, and for each other. A handful of Jesus' disciples two thousand years ago brought the transforming message of the kingdom of God to a waiting world. If today we harness the energy of values-led, mission-driven, vision-directed servant-leaders, transformation will happen in our time. But the question remains as to how best to harness that energy.

Robert Greenleaf answered the question with a story from the life of an extraordinary Quaker leader, John Woolman. By dint of his strong personality and his message, Woolman had, by 1770, created such a successful crusade against slavery among his faith community that no Quaker in the American colonies after that date owned another human being. Greenleaf, in his comments on the remarkable achievement of this single individual, goes on to speculate what our country would have become if there had been a small group made up of people like John Woolman. "One wonders," Greenleaf writes, "what would have been the result if there had been fifty John Woolmans or even five, traveling the length and breadth of the colonies in the eighteenth century persuading people, one by one, with gentle non-judgmental argument that a wrong should be righted by individual voluntary action."

In retrospect, a few John Woolmans might have transformed history so profoundly that the American Civil War would not have been inevitable, and six hundred thousand lives could have been spared. In other words, the power of even the greatest individuals can be magnified enormously when joined with others in a group effort.

How the Work of Ministry Gets Done

We believe that the work of serving others is done most effectively through teams and small groups. In fact, if we look at growing congregations in North America, and indeed throughout the world, we see that this characteristic is shared by them all. Why? Because groups and teams replicate the spiritual DNA of the congregation, especially in terms of carrying out the mission.

Now, this presents a dilemma for mainstream congregations that are often hostile to the growth of new cells, even to new groups that serve others. Even though cells are the fundamental units of congregational life, it is almost as if congregations have, as we suggested in an earlier chapter, developed antibodies to combat the concept. In the organic model, however, the congregation is not simply an *organization with* small groups, but a dynamic, living, *organism* made up *of* small groups. Because of the importance that the organic model places on cells, the congregation should celebrate, like a new birth, the beginning of new cells—ministry teams and small groups—as an affirmation of their commitment to the future.

Small Groups: The Start of Something Big

Let's first look at small groups and what they are all about; then we'll see how they can be implemented effectively by a servant-leader.

A woman approached Brent Smith, minister at All Souls Church, Tulsa, and told her story. "I was here at All Souls in the 1980s," she said, "and began going through my divorce. I knew very few people here and had to go to another congregation to find companionship. I've returned ten years later because I decided to give All Souls one more chance. If it wasn't for the [small] groups I would have had to leave again." Another person told Pastor Smith that being in a small group "is the most important thing that has ever happened to me in my life. I've discovered lifelong friendships here, people I will grow old with."

In *Sharing the Journey: Support Groups and America's New Quest for Community*, Robert Wuthnow, a professor of sociology at Princeton University, notes that "the small group movement is beginning to alter American society, both by changing our understanding of community and by redefining spirituality." Small groups have indeed made a tremendous impact, and a significant contribution not just to North American religious life but also to our cultural life.

Consider the number and types of spiritual and secular small groups already in existence: twelve-step groups, self-help groups, study groups, business planning groups, psychotherapy groups, and educational groups, to name a very few. The Church has enhanced them by adding the element of spirituality to the mix. More than anything else, the purpose of small groups is to build a sense of community, something often lacking in people's lives. Through these groups, people get to know one another, care for one another, and often reach out beyond the group to the local community.

Robert Banks and Paul Stevens comment in *The Complete Book of Everyday Christianity* that "groups give us permission to examine our faith as it relates to dilemmas of workplace, daily schedule, personal encounters, decisions, attitudes and so on. In sharing responses to these lifestyle circumstances, participants can find out what they believe, for we tend to reveal what we believe in the way we act every day. Thus small groups help us bridge from faith to life operations and back again."

What Is a Small Group?

Roberta Hestenes, former president of Eastern Theological Seminary, has given probably the most comprehensive definition of a Christian small group: "an intentional face-to-face gathering of three to ten people on a regular time schedule with the common purpose of discovering and growing in the possibilities of the abundant life in Christ." Small-group ministry, therefore, upholds the Christian tradition, reflected in Jesus' ministry of gathering people together to live out the gospel call for fellowship, worship, study, support, spiritual growth, and social change.

There are definite win-win benefits for individuals and for congregations willing to engage in small-group ministry:

- Personal spiritual growth is enhanced through encouragement, affirmation, and accountability.

- People find they are not alone, that they can give and receive support.

- New relationships and friendships are established.

- People feel a great sense of belonging.

- Lay members are equipped and empowered for genuine ministry.

- Small groups constitute the glue for caring and encouragement.

- They provide a good source and training ground for tomorrow's leaders.

- They build bridges to "unchurched" family, friends, and acquaintances.

- Churches retain members who might look elsewhere for meaningful fellowship.

- Small groups assist people in moving to the center of the life and work of the congregation.

- They help people serve each other, the congregation, and those outside the walls of the congregation.

- Small groups help participants rely on the presence of Christ to accomplish God's plan and purpose in their lives.

Small Groups Are Rooted in the Church's History

Like the concept of servant-leadership, small groups have been around for as long as the Church has been in existence. The Benedictines used them in the fourth century, the Franciscans in the thirteenth, and the Moravians in the eighteenth century.

John Wesley, the founder of Methodism, also understood the value of small groups. He realized that the good news of God's love grows and nurtures through establishing relationships in a small group, where people could gather, support each other, and be held accountable in a loving atmosphere. Today, countless people of faith are creating intentional communities where spiritual growth, personal discipleship, health and wholeness, and outreach to the larger community have become part of the riches to be derived from small-group ministry.

Five Small-Group Types

The congregation is a living organism. Just as the cells in the human body vary by function, so too do the cells (groups and teams) of a congregation. There are essentially five types:

1. Relationship-building group
2. Nurture and support group
3. Study group
4. Spiritual formation group
5. Task group (Ministry team)

Let's look at each type of small group according to its primary function.

Relationship-Building Group

Win Arn, in his concise and informative *The Church Growth Ratio Book,* concludes that a congregation has about a six-month window of opportunity to retain newcomers, who, he says, must make seven friends in six months. (We would add that this applies largely to Baby Boomers, and that the window is even smaller with Gen-Xers and Millennials. With these younger generations, the congregation must cement its relationship with them in about half the time, or three months.) Whether the time frame is six months or three months, it becomes virtually impossible to accomplish this if the newcomer's only connection with the congregation is through the worship service, even if he or she stays for the fellowship time afterward. In other words, the congregation must have ways for newcomers to build friendship networks.

Since relationship-building groups, in this context, are primarily for newcomers, wouldn't it be simpler to funnel newcomers into existing groups? Doesn't that give them a chance to meet existing congregants? Existing groups theoretically intend to include new people, but once they get under way they often develop a pattern and a rhythm that is difficult to break. Newcomers report they often feel unwelcome in existing groups and much prefer groups that include other newcomers.

Relational groups can be formed around a variety of affinities: age, neighborhood, marital status, career, hobby, parenting, movies, sports, newcomers to the congregation . . . any commonality that gives people a reason to get together and know one another. If the congregation's focus is on numerical growth as well as spiritual growth, there is probably no better way to achieve it than through relational small groups, which in effect become a kind of intentional family.

In all cases, the group must be a safe space for sharing life and faith journeys; typically they are short-term—four to seven weeks, with an opportunity to continue meeting.

Nurture and Support Group

Nurture and support groups primarily carry out the mission of the congregation by listening to and encouraging participants in their spiritual growth, encouraging them to share joys, concerns, and insights. In our busy and hurting world, there is always a need for nurture and support:

recovery Bible groups; groups for those going through various stages of grief; those battling long-term illness; mothers who need down time for relief, encouragement, and support; those seeking to heal painful memories; the twelve steps from a Christian perspective. In all these groups, people can learn from being with and listening to each other; transformation can be found in giving and receiving support.

Study Group

A study group's primary purpose is to carry out the mission of the congregation through learning together. For example, a group of young parents meet to learn specific techniques or skills of parenting. For them, information as well as relationship building are important. Education has long been a special emphasis in the mainstream congregation; however, in many of them the pastor's weekly Bible study is the only educational offering. A number of growing congregations have supplemented the weekly Bible class with study groups of all kinds, whose topics deal with social issues, spiritual and personal growth, theological exploration, family and career, and enrichment, seen from a spiritual or biblical perspective.

Isn't a study group, then, another form of class? We suggest that there are several important differences. The primary purpose of a class is for the instructor to teach and the participants to learn something. A class is typically larger, more structured, and more content-focused than a study group. Both classes and study groups, however, make real contributions to the life of the congregation.

Spiritual Formation Group

Spiritual formation is a process of personal growth and development that begins when a person encounters and enters into a relationship with God. One is transformed, "the old has gone, the new has come" (2 Corinthians 5:17 NIV). "Melt me, mold me, fill me, use me" reads the familiar hymn. Spiritual molding and shaping—spiritual formation—are part of the ongoing process of this deepening relationship with God.

There has been an exciting rediscovery of the power of God working in one's life. The guidance of a spiritual director; the insights gained during a retreat; educational experiences, such as the Alpha Course; and the daily use of devotional materials all assist in the process. Increasingly, people are becoming involved in small lay-led groups that foster spiritual growth and accountability in daily life. These formation groups provide an environment in which growth and development toward a defined target can occur through study, life application, and accountability.

Task Group (Ministry Team)

Ministry teams are small groups that organize to accomplish a specific task. In *The Wisdom of Teams,* Jon Katzenbach and Doug Smith define a team as "a small number of people with complementary skills who are committed to a common purpose, performance goals, and approach for which they hold themselves mutually accountable." This is also a good definition of a task group.

Early Christians formed task teams for effective ministry. Paul and Barnabas, as a team, went to Antioch to support the newly formed body of believers there. Later, they went on a missionary journey for the church at Antioch to bring the good news to the gentiles. In each instance, Paul and Barnabas organized task teams to ensure that their work would be carried forward when they left.

Jesus' disciples accompanied him on his journeys and witnessed firsthand how he ministered to people. Then he sent them out on practice missions in which they followed his example. When they returned, he listened and coached them. Jesus gave them their "basic training"; when he was no longer physically with them, from their experience of him they too formed teams.

The ministry team is an ideal way to do the work of God and can take many forms, ranging from high-level decision making (by a board, the trustees, or a council) to teams of ushers, greeters, hospitality people; from a choir to a sacred arts team, altar workers, and others. We can't overemphasize the importance of individual and group buy-in on the part of the team. People must be willing to work together in mutual accountability and trust, in which they recognize that diversity of personality, skills, and gifts is itself a gift.

Teamwork brings a number of obvious benefits to the congregation and the participants:

- Working together, it's easier to achieve excellence.

- A team facilitates learning even in a chaotic and rapidly changing environment, thus making it easier to deal with unforeseen needs.

- A team shares performance goals or results; its members are accountable to each other.

- A team is self-directed, self-managed, and flexible; therefore it can involve more people in ministry.

- The greatest benefit of team ministry is that it opens the way for individuals to grow spiritually while being in intentional community with others.

A Mix of LLDD

Henry Miller once commented, "Spiritual growth is an individual affair that is best pursued in groups." A true small group is where people gather in heart-to-heart fellowship and learn to care for one another. To accomplish this, each small group or team ideally embodies LLDD, a mix of four action components (love, learn, do, decide). They operate within the context of a spiritual environment, no matter what type of small group it is.

Group members *love*. They care for one another and share in each other's lives through accountability, prayer, and intentional acts of service.

They *learn*, experiencing a growing knowledge of God and of themselves.

The members *do* some duties that serve people inside as well as outside the group.

They *make decisions* about the group's activities, scheduling, and agreements.

The preponderance of one or more of these components varies with the nature of the group. However, all groups use all four components complementarily. For example, in a relationship-building group love is the major component. In a book study group, learning is the chief component. In a support group, nurture is the primary focus. A spiritual formation group may emphasize practices that promote Christian living and accountability. Finally, of course, task groups stress doing the work of the congregation. Yet with all these groups and teams, the mix of love, learn, do, and decide is always present.

Mainstream Churches and Small Groups

Cell-based, organic, small-group ministry with its potential to replicate not only produces the largest churches in our country (and in the world, for that matter) but also yields the healthiest congregations. Moreover, teams and small groups are an excellent way to put servant-leadership into practice. Having said that, why does it appear so difficult for an existing mainstream congregation to develop truly effective small-group ministry?

Certainly, most mainstream congregations would like to have a successful small-group ministry. Many have tried and were unsuccessful. Why? Here are a few observations:

- They don't perceive the strategic importance of small-group ministry. It's seen as implementing just another program.

- Most congregations are heavily curriculum-oriented; something must be learned, or why else meet? Thus a group that is intended solely for relationship building, support, or nurture is alien.

- Committees and commissions have become so pervasive in mainstream congregations that self-organizing, self-regulating, short-term groups are a challenging concept.

- Current groups really do not want newcomers. "They disturb our intimacy" is the usual comment, or "They're not like us."

So what can be done?

- Communicate to the congregation why and how small-group ministry is an important way to carry out your mission—that is, the group is significant to your primary task, which is transformation.

- Start off gradually. Introduce small groups through the Spiritual Explorers Class, or through a new-members class.

- Use a small group as part of your follow-up activity for a Big Sunday event, and for other special events, workshops, and seminars.

- Allow volunteers who have ideas and passions for new ministry activities to start a new group.

Small Group FAQs

Before you plunge into forming your groups, let's look at some of the basic elements that make small groups work. These include group size, meeting place, and other guidelines. Here are a few of the most frequently asked questions posed to us.

How Big Should a Small Group Be?

Ideally, a group should number no more than twelve, including the three who form the nucleus of the group (the leader, an assistant leader, and sometimes a host). This leaves nine or ten places to be filled. How they are filled depends on the nature of your group. If this is an in-house group intended for members of the congregation, you fill it from their ranks.

If your group is intended for numerical growth, the process is a bit different. In this case, no more than four of the spaces should be filled with incorporated members of the congregation, and the remaining spaces filled with newcomers. Obviously, for greater growth, the more spaces filled by newcomers the better.

Must a Curriculum Be Followed?

In a permission-giving environment, this is up to you and the person who brings the group into existence. Some small groups get along just fine by posing a leading question and letting the group discuss it. Others prefer an ordered curriculum with specific topics. Some groups prefer to develop their own curriculum according to their needs. We encourage you to discern what method best meets the needs of the participants.

Where Should the Group Meet?

Small groups meet anywhere people conveniently gather: a home, an apartment, a community room, a church room, a restaurant, and so on. Generally, they meet in private homes, for several reasons. A home promotes greater informality with its natural setting. A residence eases one-to-one interaction and is comfortable for those who are not yet ready to feel at home in other settings.

How Often Should the Group Meet, and for How Long?

Preferably, meetings are held each week, or at least every other week. It is difficult to build relationships if a group meets less frequently. Meetings are typically one or two hours in length. Lengthy meetings (over two hours) tend to create mental and physical fatigue. Shorter meetings (less than an hour) do not allow enough time to accomplish the purpose of the meeting.

Should the Group Begin and End on Time?

Yes! More and more people are running their lives by their Day Timers, so it is important to stick to the established time agreement. If a group develops a pattern of late starting, the start time grows progressively later. Everyone should be encouraged to be on time. If refreshments are served before the meeting, members soon learn that if they're late they'll miss the goodies. Regardless of how well the meeting is going, it should close at the agreed-upon time. Going into overtime is unfair to those who have to leave on schedule.

Should Groups Be Open to Newcomers?

Opening up a group to newcomers depends on the culture of your congregation, and the purpose of the group. However, if your groups are intended to increase the congregation numerically, they should for obvious reasons be open. To symbolize the fact that newcomers are welcome, an empty chair is traditionally included. The facilitator should remind participants at each meeting that newcomers are welcome. In a couples group, two empty chairs might be included. Caution should be exercised to avoid any appearance of closing off a group to newcomers, especially if the old refrain is voiced that "our intimacy will be disturbed." If not checked through constant reinforcement, this groundless fear effectively kills off a small-group ministry. There is always room for one more person to come into a small group to find healing for his or her life and to begin building dreams for the future.

How Long Should a Group Stay Together?

There is no one answer to this question. A group should continue to meet for as long as it fulfills the mission or purpose. Some groups have been known to stay together for as long as two years, and others have gone on even longer, while most are complete in a shorter period of time.

How Will People Learn About Our Small Groups?

There are many ways to inform people about your small group(s). Here are just a few. The pastor talks about them on Sundays. Create a brochure or flyer and include it on the information table. Make oral announcements during the service. Place written announcements in the program. Create a small-group bulletin board, include names and locations of groups, and provide pictures of leaders and snapshots of group sessions. Once the group has started, brief testimony from participants about the power of the small group might be made during Sunday services. Schedule regular orientation sessions to explain small groups, and to sign folks up. Provide sign-up sheets after worship services with the name and purpose of your small group, and directions to the host site. Include a short small-group session in a new-members class to introduce people to the concept. The best method of course, is a direct one-on-one invitation.

What Are Small Groups Called?

Small groups are given many designations. Here are just some of the names congregations have used:

Covenant and care group	Life flow group
Connections circle	Practical spirituality group
TLC group	Positive living circle
Enrichment circle	Empowerment group
ShareCarePrayer group	Loving care circle
Circle of love	Quest group
Shepherd group	Friendship circle
Base community	Heart-to-heart group
Relationship circle	Home group
Christ circle	Life enrichment group
Kerygma group	

Starting a Small-Group Ministry

Now that you've learned the types of small groups and their importance in the life of the congregation, you can begin to form your own
small-group ministry (see Exhibit 6.1). It can be as simple or as complex as you choose to make it. The simpler the procedure of getting
groups up and running, the more effective they probably will be.

Small-group ministry is most effective when there are trained
people leading the groups. One of the best training procedures is
the apprenticeship model. Potential leaders learn by participating
in an actual small group and observing the leader in action. Initially,
this might be any servant-leader who has previously had the experience of being in a small group or has served as a small-group leader
and wants to empower others to become leaders.

Ongoing Training and Support:
An Essential Component

The church world, like the world of management, has found that leaders who are supported and offered training can make a difference in
strengthening the serving system. Robert Hargrove comments, in his
Masterful Coaching Fieldbook, that the leader "works with people to
create a shared vision and values based on what matters to the institution, its demands and constraints, and what the people passionately
care about." Adequate training helps to develop practical skills that
aid the leader in the ministry opportunity. A frequent mistake is to
assume that an individual is capable of taking on a particular task if
someone simply tells the person what to do. What's the possible result?
People end up serving in ministry areas for which they have no expertise and little preparation, or in which they have not been gifted.

Support is also a necessary component. Occasional gatherings of
leaders, where they can share joys and concerns, victories and challenges, questions and solutions with others who are involved in leading groups and teams is important. We suggest monthly or bimonthly
meetings, with ongoing support and training. At a typical meeting,

Exhibit 6.1. Sample Agenda for a Small-Group Meeting

Arrange the chairs in a circle with one *empty chair* as a constant
reminder that the group is open to others.

Leader's Opening Comments
The leader opens the meeting with prayer:

> Welcome to our small group. Let's begin by introducing ourselves
> by name and briefly share one thing that you are grateful for
> today (this week, this month, etc.).

Setting the Context
The leader (or someone else) comments that Jesus said to the people, "If
you have faith no larger than a mustard-seed, you could tell this mountain
to move from here to there. And it would. Everything would be possible
for you" (Matthew 17:20).

Questions for Discussion and Sharing
1. When did faith become more than just a word for you?
2. Describe an experience that has strengthened your faith?
3. Is faith alone enough? Does faith need "feet?"

Affirmation
At the end of the discussion and sharing time, each participant turns to
the person on his or her left and says (addressing the person by name),
"_____, God has a purpose for your life that will be a blessing to
the world."

Closing
The leader closes the meeting with a prayer.

---

the pastor reminds the folks about why they have committed to this
ministry. The group then breaks into small discussion groups in
which leaders discuss their activities and address challenges that
have come up in their groups, as well as possible solutions. After the
group discussions, everyone reconvenes to focus on a particular skill
intended to assist them in being effective leaders.

Recognition: "Well Done, Good and Faithful Servant"

All servant-leaders, including all small-group leaders and participants on ministry teams, should be recognized by a grateful congregation. Honoring volunteers is a top priority, and demonstrating gratitude goes a long way to building good and long-lasting relationships.

The medieval mystic Meister Eckhart said, "The most powerful prayer of all is when we say thank you." Yet "thank you" are two words that are underused in many congregations. We think it's because congregations assume people know they are appreciated. But if people don't receive some form of recognition, they'll assume they are *not* appreciated. We all have a very human need to be acknowledged for what we've done. It's not just a one-shot occurrence; it must be done over and over, in many ways. Michael Murray, pastor and church consultant, talks about the need for "psychic pay" for volunteers. He says that volunteers need to know that the congregation considers them and their efforts worthwhile. It's critical to the success of any volunteer program that you look for opportunities to let people know how much you value them.

Recognition should be on two levels, personal and public. On a personal level, authentically praising individuals or groups for some aspect of their work enhances your program and supports the honored individuals to do more—and you'll feel good for taking this action. Margie Morris writes in *Volunteer Ministries*, "Recognition does more than express appreciation. It validates. It motivates. It provides both incentive and visibility to the volunteer." You will be saying to the volunteers that their work is important and that the congregation supports their efforts.

Public recognition is a way of saying, "Well done, good and faithful servant," in the presence of the congregation. Hebrews 10:24 (TM) says, "Let's see how inventive we can be in encouraging love and helping out . . . spurring others on. . . . " Here are five basic possibilities; you can probably add five more.

1. List all volunteers in the Sunday program and the newsletter. Occasionally profile a volunteer who has done something outstanding. Display their pictures.

2. Develop special recognition certificates.

3. Create a special lay ministry cover for the Sunday service program.

4. Write and send articles to your local newspaper highlighting a few volunteers, emphasizing how they have made a difference in the community.

5. Plan a special "lay ministry night" to honor volunteers. This could include worship, food, sharing, and some form of talent show.

Let's take a brief look at how one congregation handles recognition of volunteer workers.

The parish has a part-time pastor and relies heavily on volunteer service. Though the parish is small, its budget contains a sizable allocation to honor volunteers. They do it each year through an elegantly catered dinner and dance at a local hotel. Everyone is honored by name, and each year a particular volunteer activity is singled out for special mention. An emcee pokes good-natured fun at the activity, and they follow it up with skits and songs.

Then comes the time for one tradition that they've kept for years. It's one they look forward to and wouldn't change for the world. As dessert is served, each person is given a small wrapped gift. The pastor then says, "Scripture tells us that the laborer is worthy of his and her hire. And though you are volunteers, and you do it out of your love for God and for our congregation, you have a right to at least one pay day. So, here it is, please open your gifts." Well, they all know exactly what's inside, yet gales of laughter roll across the room as each person unwraps a PayDay candy bar!

Sharing the Opportunities

As a rule, we recommend that no volunteer be involved in more than two activities—one that feeds him or her spiritually, and one where the person feeds others spiritually. This prevents burnout and decreases the possibility of controlling interests successfully closing off opportunities. The circle of participation should always be drawn wider by opening up space for new volunteers and for new creative ideas.

This is quite different from the prevailing method of asking a small, reliable, and increasingly exhausted core group to shoulder ever more of the load. In this busy world we inhabit, giving of oneself to one ministry activity with enthusiasm and commitment to quality is important. By the same token, learning to receive nurture from others is just as important. Simply following this procedure of feeding others through one ministry activity and being fed through one other lessens the burden on already overworked volunteers, dismantles the personal fiefdoms of select laity, and opens up opportunity for new volunteers.

We believe that service, especially through a team or small group, invites people into purposeful ministry where their God-given skills and passions can assist others in their spiritual growth, and in the process deepen their personal relationship with God. What we are saying in no way negates the value of a single individual who wishes to serve the congregation. We are suggesting that when leaders join together to serve God and others, their ability to serve is strengthened enormously. Servant-leadership, expressed through teams and small groups, truly reflects Jesus' call, "If anyone wants to be first, he must be the very last, and the servant of all."

Part III

The Strategic Mapping Process

I will bless you with a future filled with hope—a future of success . . .
Jeremiah 29:11

High above a doorway to an ancient shrine in the Greek city of Delphi is an inscription that captures the essence of spiritual DNA: "Know thyself." To renew and grow, a congregation must know itself: its identity, its purpose for being, and the significant values and beliefs that it holds.

Through self-knowledge, decisions about mission and ministry are made that reflect the highest response to God's call. In the gospel, self-knowledge is a dynamic process of accepting and reaccepting a new identity derived from the good news that God calls us to rebirth through healing, reconciliation, freedom, wholeness, and justice.

Through self-knowledge, the community of faith can answer, with wisdom and faith, Jesus' call for *metanoia*—life change rooted in God's gift of new awareness and discernment. This type of self-knowing comes essentially through understanding the spiritual inner geography of a congregation, and then mapping this terrain with fresh objectivity.

7

Creating Your Strategic Map to Take You Where You Want to Go

S trategic mapping is a journey, not a destination. We live in a world of maps and words that can be helpful as navigational tools to point us in the right direction toward our true identity as the body of Christ, but we should not confuse the maps and the words with the identity. Strategic mapping is the process by which you detail your congregation's inner geography and indicate how you will act on that information. It's a description of how you intend to get from where you are now to where you want to be in the future.

The question strategic mappers ask themselves is, "What can we do today that brings into reality God's vision for our future?" The journey of discovery you take in response to this question can be uncomfortable, but it can also be powerful and exciting. In mapping the answer, the congregation must confront the tenacity of its ingrained habits, hidden agendas, and resistance to God's newness. This is because strategic mapping is about change. When a congregation embarks on change, it discovers just what kind of stake it has in maintaining the status quo. If we are used to operating within certain paradigms—as we have in the Church for centuries—it's easy to see why change can be a long, difficult, and frustrating process because it upsets the established order.

Strategic mapping helps to break new ground and to learn how to think and act differently, which is known as a paradigm shift. A paradigm is a set of rules and regulations that establish boundaries; it is within those boundaries that problem solving takes place. The current paradigm—the one we accept and operate under—acts as a filter that screens data as they come into our minds. It determines not only *how* we see things but *what* we see, and it governs how we think and interpret. Once an interpretation has been accepted, it becomes a reality for us. We become so accustomed to our own mind-set that we don't usually allow ourselves space to question it. When challenged, we respond, "That's the way it is."

Or when we're questioned about a particular practice, we are likely to answer, "That's the way we've always done it." We can't see what we're doing because to do so requires stepping outside of the paradigm. But when a paradigm shift does occur, it's as if a curtain has been lifted. It *appears* that nothing has changed, but the shift allows us to see the same things differently. This is a valuable asset for strategic mappers.

We see eight key steps in creating your strategic map:

1. Form a vision team.
2. Discern your congregation's values.
3. Write a mission statement.
4. Create your vision of a new tomorrow.
5. Strengthen the four systems.
6. Decide whom you will serve.
7. Create ministry pathways.
8. State your goals and objectives.

Form a Vision Team

Strategic mapping is the job of a *vision team,* a small group of servant-leaders who have been empowered to envision—to dream about the future of the congregation and how it can carry out its mission in new and creative ways. Ultimately, the vision team is responsible for creating and committing the strategic map to paper (see the outline at the end of this chapter).

The vision team members should be representative of the congregation—five to twenty-five people, depending on the size of the congregation. The members of the team include the pastor and key leaders, as well those who support the growth of the congregation: regular attenders, new people, young people, older folks, and those in between. People who have not participated in the past often step forward to be on a vision team. Although the team makes a commitment to the strategic mapping process over a number of months, it does not work in a vacuum. As a living whole, and as a part of the greater whole, the team frequently communicates with the congregation. Interaction between the team and the faith community is necessary; without this open communication, you would guarantee conflict and suspicion.

To summarize, a vision team:

- Is empowered by and acts on behalf of the congregation

- Communicates to the congregation current information on renewal and growth

- Identifies strategies and tactics to carry out the mission effectively

- Recommends to decision makers, through a strategic map, activities to implement their recommendations

- Allows its members to serve as resource persons as the implementation process is engaged

The role of the vision team ends once the strategic map has been adopted by the congregation. At this point, we suggest that a *vision implementation team* be constituted, whose task is to coordinate, initiate, and monitor the changes detailed in the map.

Discern Your Congregation's Values

Core values help you sort out what's really important, what your congregation stands for. Values form the basis for developing policies and procedures, for creating cohesiveness and teamwork, and for developing ministry activities. They guide you in conflict resolution and decision making; they help you decide where to invest your time, your energy, and your resources. They bolster strength and guidance in good times and bad. Core values tell you not only what you can do but also what you should *not* do.

During this discernment process, your vision team *identifies*, *defines*, and *prioritizes* your core values. Then it narrows them down until they get to those values that represent the core of what your congregation stands for. It takes time, but in the long run the effort helps you achieve a high level of clarity. Finally, the team *shares* these core values with the congregation.

Identify Your Values

What are core values? *Core* means "a central, often foundational part." *Value* comes from the root word *valor*, which means "something intrinsically valuable or desirable." Your core values are those foundational, deeply rooted beliefs and strengths that impel you to take action. They are so important that your mission, your vision, and all your ministry activities must be in alignment with them.

Activity

What is important to your congregation? Take some time for the team to reflect on these five questions. Have the members write out their answers, either individually or in groups. Discuss them.

1. How would you define the fundamental character of your congregation?

2. What brings meaning to the life and work of your congregation?

3. What is so important, so vital, to your congregation that you wouldn't, under any circumstances, change it?

4. What factors influence the decisions you make?

5. What factors are necessary to generate a meaningful and productive atmosphere?

Ranking Values

As part of the next exercise, you are asked to rank your values. We often hear the concern, especially in mainstream congregations, that the very act of ranking opposes openness and inclusion. Ken Wilber, in his book *One Taste,* answers this objection: "If you don't like values rankings and want to avoid them, then fine, *that* is your value ranking—you rank nonranking as better than ranking—and that itself is a ranking, your ranking. . . . The fact is, ranking is unavoidable in values, so at least do it consciously, honestly, and above board."

Now, you and the vision team are ready to begin the process. Distribute the core values survey in Exhibit 7.1 to all participants.

Define and Prioritize Your Values

Define, in sentence form, what these values mean in the context of your congregation. There are at least two ways you can do this. You can meet as a team and work out each definition. Or you can break into subteams, with each subteam taking a core value to define and bringing its results to the whole team for discussion and refinement.

Now, *prioritize* them. Yes, this means in 1, 2, 3 order (as Jesus and Paul did; see Chapters One and Two).

Share Your Values with the Congregation

It is important, and judicious, to keep the congregation in the loop. We recommend that once the core values have been identified, defined, and prioritized, the vision team should implement a "feedback mechanism" for the congregation. Here are five suggested ways.

A Picture Is Worth a Thousand Words

Create a poster for each core value with a collage of pictures illustrating the value. Add a few phrases that express the vision team's understanding of the value. Display them in the church narthex or

Exhibit 7.1. Core Values Survey

1. Look over the values listed in these three columns. Which of the values do you personally feel your congregation should display? Rank all of the values according to the scale. There are blank lines for others not listed.

    Scale: 1 = very important 2 = important 3 = not so important

____ Pleasure	____ Diplomacy	____ Teamwork
____ Health	____ Friendship	____ Neatness
____ Challenge	____ Respectfulness	____ Rationality
____ Adventure	____ Helping	____ Perseverance
____ Personal growth	____ Appearance	____ Tradition
____ Creativity	____ Family	____ Self-control
____ Spiritual growth	____ Prosperity	____ Belonging
____ Self-acceptance	____ Play	____ Consensus
____ Knowledge	____ Intimacy	____ Competence
____ Inner harmony	____ Passion	____ Recognition
____ Honesty	____ Integrity	____ Intellectual status
____ Environment	____ Peace	____ Achievement
____ Courage	____ Forgiveness	____ Authority
____ Security	____ Fairness	____ Competition
____ Stability	____ Tolerance	____ Diversity
____ Power	____ Communication	____ Justice
____ _____	____ _____	____ _____

2. Now ask each participant to look over his or her "very important" values, narrow them down to five that seem most important, and list them on the sheet.

3. Tally the group's responses in one of two ways:
    *   Collect all of the values exercise sheets and tally the "very important" values on a master sheet; or
    *   Go around the vision team and ask each individual to read out their chosen "very important" values responses, while a scribe ticks

them off on a master sheet. Then tally the totals, and list the
values chosen on chart paper.

4. Narrow the list down. Poll the vision team once more, asking them
to vote for three to five of the values you've listed on the chart paper.
When everyone has spoken, tally the counts. Then circle those
values with the highest counts. You want at least three, but no more
than five. These are your core values.

---

in the main fellowship area. Provide colored stick-on dots or labels.
Ask the congregation to indicate which of these values, as pictured
through the collages, they respond to most by placing a label, or a
check mark, on the poster. Leave the posters up for a few weeks to
allow as many people as possible to participate. After an appropriate time, count the number of dots (check marks) and you'll have
their feedback.

Do the Entire Core Values Survey

Give advance notice to the congregation, and on a Sunday, either
as part of or after the service, administer the entire core values survey of Exhibit 7.1 to those in attendance. Gather the surveys, collate the responses, and report the results the following week.

Have the Congregation Prioritize

Give the congregation a listing of the core values the team has
identified and defined, and ask the congregants to prioritize them.
Once you collate and count them, you'll have their sense of a values prioritization.

Preach the Core Values

The pastor preaches a message, or a series of messages, on the importance of core values in the life of the congregation. (A number of our
client congregations have audiotaped and packaged these talks as a
series and then used them as an introduction to the congregation for

newcomers. Or the packaged series could be offered to members to purchase for themselves or as gifts for their loved ones and friends.)

Communicate Your Values

The vision team reports on what these core values mean to the life of the congregation:

- During a worship service

- In the worship program or bulletin

- At committee meetings

- In the newsletter, by direct mail, or by e-mail

Using the Other Values Rankings

Three categories were included in the rankings: "very important," "important," and "not as important." We recommended concentrating on the very important values in the initial process. It would, however, be useful for the team to consider the other categories as well. You might prioritize both of those categories to give you an even clearer sense of your congregation's value system.

Write a Mission Statement

Your values answer the question, "What is important for us?" Your mission is the central organizing principle of your congregation. It describes your purpose—your rationale—for being. At the heart of your mission is the transformation of individuals and the community.

Consider this mission statement: "We are called to be a diverse and inclusive community of Christians in the Anglican tradition. We offer a compassionate haven for reconciliation, spiritual growth, and commitment to social justice."

This is an excellent statement. It clearly indicates the congregation's identity ("a diverse and inclusive community of Christians"). It

includes its inherited identity ("in the Anglican tradition"). This congregation understands itself to be "a compassionate haven" as its key
to spiritual transformation. It offers transformation through three broad
ministry pathways ("reconciliation, spiritual growth, and commitment
to social justice"). All the essential components of a viable mission,
as laid out in Chapter Two, are contained in one succinct statement.

Let's turn now to the actual process of writing your congregation's mission statement. First ask your vision team to answer these
questions one at a time:

1. Describe your congregation. Who are you as a community
   of faith?

2. What is your "offer" of transformation?

3. How do you intend to carry this out?

Say everything that needs to be said. You are looking for
insights, not polished statements. Don't move on until you feel that
your replies are complete. Write down comments and ideas on chart
paper. If your group is large, break into three groups and assign one
question to each group. The groups can work independently and
then, when the whole team reassembles, each can report on its work
and get feedback from the others.

The second step is to take your responses to the first question
and combine them into a one-paragraph summary. Follow this
process with the responses to the second and third questions. Next,
get to the essence of your comments by striking out of the para-
graphs all extraneous words and phrases that don't alter the central
theme. Reduce each paragraph to a single sentence.

With this as your basis, go on to compose the sentences into a preliminary statement that clearly conveys who you are and what you
are about. Here's a hint: a mission statement contains strong *verbs*.
We recommend designating an individual, or a subteam, to do the
actual crafting of your statement. Group writing is not productive,

and it can take an inordinate amount of time. Your mission statement should be (1) no longer than one or two sentences, (2) easily understood by anyone above the age of twelve, and (3) easy to recite from memory.

A mission slogan, if you choose to have one, is either a condensation of the mission statement or a few key words that capture the essence of the statement.

As a matter of prudence, the vision team should be sure some mechanism for feedback from the congregation is in place.

Create Your Vision of a New Tomorrow

Your values present the context of the journey, and your mission the purpose of the journey. Your vision is the picture of where your congregation is headed. A vision is a desired future reality, a powerful image of what you want to create in the future. It should capture the hearts and minds of the congregation in such a compelling way that they are willing to commit their time, talent, and treasure to make it a reality. Creating a shared vision based on your core values can be a slow process, but not a difficult one.

Consider this example of a vision statement: "Our vision is to share our belief in God and God's love. We welcome all people to our mutually supportive, loving congregation. We envision a cohesive, vital church community with wise stewardship of our resources, and spiritually enriching worship. Our vision encompasses our own renewal and growth, individually, as families, and as a congregation, through serving each other and the greater community."

This statement is powerful because it describes clearly this congregation's view of what a transformed faith community looks like. As with all good vision statements, this is an overarching picture of transformation. Note that no specific activities that would carry the congregation in the direction of the vision are listed. These are found in your goals and objectives, which we discuss in the last of the eight key steps in creating your strategic map.

Setting the Context

Before you begin the process, remind the vision team that they are forming a specific vision for the future; in this process they describe what the future will look like, on the basis of your values and your mission.

Your vision statement should:

- Be realistic, credible, well articulated, and easy to understand

- Focus on the energies of the congregation, and inspire it to achieve its mission

- Be consistent with its values

- Describe, by painting word pictures in the present tense, your ideal future

- Be responsive to change (you are always able to add new pictures or amend old ones)

"Dream the Possible Dream" Activity

This group activity is a great way to jump-start your visioning process.

To begin, give each participant a pack of four-by-six index cards ("dream cards") and a felt-tip pen. (As an alternative, use a flipchart and make it a group process. Or put up sheets of chart paper on the walls and let people jot down their dreams when they are ready.)

Create a time line on a large sheet of paper. On the left side, write the current date, and at the far end write a date three, four, or five years in the future. We suggest that you begin by going backward in the dream process, from the end date to the present. Why? Because if you start with the current date you might get stuck in the current realities and find it difficult to get past them. Starting at the end date lets you look to the future, to where you want to go, and then proceed back to the present.

Now you have two dates with lots of blank space in between. Ask the participants to imagine that they are in the future and that they have created the best congregation there is. What does it look like? Ask them to write on the cards what it is they see—one dream per card—in the present tense, as if it already is. Remind them not to assume that things will stay the same as they now are; they should be open to dramatic changes.

Allow people the space to dream; it may take some a while to warm up to the process. Every once in a while, ask someone to read a dream card as a means of inspiring the others.

As people complete a dream card, they affix it on the time line. During the process, encourage people to get up and scan the cards that are posted.

Narrow the Dream

Break up into groups, and begin the process of consolidating the dream cards. If two people have more or less the same dream cards, try to combine them into one. Narrow down the range of content of the cards as specifically as possible. Or gather all of the cards and let the team, or a subteam, combine similar dreams into as few cards as possible, and narrow the cards down till you discern some specific visions of the future.

What Are the Obstacles?

Dreaming the possible dream is a wonderful exercise, but it must be tempered by reality. In your dreaming, consider the obstacles on the way to fulfillment, and how they may be overcome. This too is part of visioning.

Craft a Preliminary Vision Statement

As we recommended earlier, try not to write your vision statement as a group project. Ask one or two people to draft a preliminary statement and bring it back to the group. Revise it until you have something that you can agree upon and that your leaders can share with enthusiasm.

Now, begin finalizing your vision. This is the wordsmiths' heaven, so let them take over. Vision statements are written in the present tense; use *nouns and pronouns* and descriptive details that anchor it to reality. Your preliminary statement should identify no more than three to five ministry areas that you feel God is calling you to create or to strengthen. It isn't necessary for you to think of everything right at the start; details can be added later. Nor should your vision statement be a catch-all for everything the congregation would like to do.

Although a vision statement can be several pages long, if you want it to be effective and readily noticed by others keep it short and to the point. A succinctly worded statement can be empowering, motivating, and inspiring. If the vision team isn't inspired by it, your congregation probably won't be either.

Share, Change, and Finalize

Once you've honed the vision down to a clear, concise statement, share it with the congregation. Let them know it is a preliminary statement, and that their input is wanted. After you've allowed sufficient time for feedback, allow the wordsmiths to incorporate the changes into the statement. Keep it simple, keep it exciting, keep it to the point. Your final steps are to have the vision approved by the proper judicatory, print it, and distribute it widely around the congregation.

Strengthen the Four Systems

You have cracked your congregation's code. You have a new, deep understanding of your spiritual DNA: your core values, mission, and vision. Honestly evaluating the health of your welcoming, nurturing, empowering, and serving systems gives you a clear picture of your current situation, that is, how well this DNA is presently being delivered throughout the organism.

To map the health of these systems:

1. Scan the current strengths and weaknesses of the systems.
2. Design and introduce tactical changes to bolster the vibrancy and health of the systems.
3. Monitor the systems to test the efficacy of the changes.

Scanning, Designing, and Monitoring the Health of Your Four Systems

In this chapter, we give you basic evaluative tools that we have used with hundreds of congregations. The evaluative surveys—we call them quotients—help assess the health of your welcoming, nurturing, empowering, and serving systems. Each individual member of the vision team should complete these surveys, and then the team's responses should be collated and tabulated. The combined total gives you a clear picture of the current health of each system.

Once you have evaluated your congregational health, the team's task is to make a strategic decision to implement those tactics you feel would create greater health for the system. We suggest that you commit to some number within the "optimally healthy" range suggested in the surveys. We also recommend that you begin to look at your systems with fresh eyes, to see things as the people new to the congregation might see them. Finally, establish a timetable with specific implementation dates, and name the people in the group or team who are responsible for implementation.

Monitoring the health of the systems should become a regular function in the life of the congregation. To do this, form a *vision implementation team* to initiate and coordinate the systemic changes. The team should revisit the systems periodically—every six months is a good time frame—to determine if some aspect of your strategic map needs to be altered. If, for example, the team finds that a particular tactic has not made the system healthier, they have the option to modify or even abandon the tactic. They should be aware that changes introduced into the genetic makeup are not magic; they need ample time to take effect.

Example: Implementing the Process

It's one matter to agree that things need to change; it's quite another to figure out *what* needs to change and how to do it. To discern an appropriate tactical change, the vision team should implement the process in three steps. Let's take a close look at these important components of the mapping process:

1. Having assessed the current health of the system, identify the challenge.
2. Determine what steps might be taken to alleviate the challenge.
3. Introduce the new tactics that reflect your strategies.

Let's study a specific example—an overstuffed Sunday service program—to see how these three steps can be implemented.

Identify the Challenge

The Sunday service program has become cumbersome and unwieldy. From the layout of the program, people find the service difficult to follow. On top of that, the program is packed with loose inserts announcing new activities; every group wants its insert included. Ushers report that the majority of the programs are simply left in the pews after the service. The cleaning crew says that most of the loose inserts, which have fallen out of the programs, end up on the floor.

Determine the Appropriate Action

As the team thinks about the problem strategically, they ask themselves, *What is our purpose in producing this Sunday service program?* It is, they realize, to serve the mission and vision of the congregation effectively through providing information. Is it doing that? The team starts asking questions and listening. They find that people are so overwhelmed with the amount of information in the program that few actually read it all. They learn that folks think the program is "too busy," unattractive, and difficult to follow. They also acquire some additional information: that not everyone can easily find their way around the facilities.

Introduce the New Tactics

On the basis of the information received, the team designs a new format for the program. It's a clean design, there is more white space, and the new font is easier to read. They replace the confusing system of asterisks (*) they have been using with plain English words: "stand," "sit," "kneel," and so on. The words to the songs are printed out. Basic texts (such as the Lord's Prayer) that everyone repeats are printed out fully.

Additionally, they read through the program and circle any words or phrases that newcomers might not understand. Then they take things one step further and circle words and phrases they—the regular members of the congregation—say they don't understand, and replace them with standard English. If "churchy" words are necessary, they agree to provide a brief explanation (for example, "Doxology in Greek literally means 'words of glory.' A doxology is, therefore, a glorification of God").

Newcomers, and those unfamiliar with the facilities, are assisted by the addition of a site map to the program, indicating key areas of the complex (the nursery, Sunday School rooms, restrooms, kitchen, fellowship hall, and meeting rooms). To cut down on the bulk of the program, they decide to print only announcements of general interest, or specific announcements that apply to everyone.

To ensure that adequate information is made available, they set up tables in strategic locations where all recognized groups and organizations of the congregation can leave their printed announcements; they also set up large bulletin boards as an additional means of getting the word out. They request funding for the cost of mailings, so that all recognized groups of the congregation have an additional way of reaching their particular constituents.

What's Your Evaluative Quotient?

The surveys shown in Exhibit 7.2 help you evaluate the "health" of your systems.

Exhibit 7.2. Surveys of the Four Systems

SURVEY ONE

Scan for Your Welcoming Quotient
Scan the current health of your welcoming system through this Welcoming Quotient (WQ) survey. Circle Y (yes) if you feel you implement an item or N (no) if you feel you do not. Not sure? Move on to the next one. List Y and N totals at the end of the survey.

1. Y N Are your outdoor signs visible, eye-catching, informative, properly placed, and easy to read, especially as one drives by?
2. Y N Is there activity outside your church on Sunday morning that indicates an alive congregation to those who pass or drive by?
3. Y N Do you have clearly marked visitor parking close to the church?
4. Y N Do you greet people—especially newcomers—outside the church building (in the parking lot, for example) before the service?
5. Y N Do you distinguish between hosts/greeters and ushers?
6. Y N Do you require training of all hosts/greeters and ushers?
7. Y N Do you include children accompanying adults as hosts/greeters and ushers?
8. Y N Do you have an easy-access information center that includes *welcoming* materials for newcomers?
9. Y N Do you provide a thank-you remembrance for newcomers?

(Continued)

Exhibit 7.2. Continued

10. Y N   Is your Sunday program easy to follow and relatively free of church jargon?

11. Y N   Do you have a quality sound system in your worship space?

12. Y N   Are restrooms, nursery, Sunday School, and other rooms clearly indicated by signs, as well as listed in the program?

13. Y N   Do you provide baby-changing stations in women's and men's restrooms?

14. Y N   Is your welcome for newcomers separated from announcements?

15. Y N   Does the sermon or message focus on the relevance of the topic to everyday life?

16. Y N   Do trained "aisle hosts" welcome newcomers after the service?

17. Y N   Are directions to the after-service social hour provided (in the program or verbally)?

18. Y N   Do your notices and bulletin boards reflect the life and work of your community of faith?

19. Y N   Do you provide for physically challenged persons and the hearing-challenged during the worship celebrations?

20. Y N   Do children participate actively in the worship experience at least several Sundays a year?

21. Y N   Is drama occasionally included in your worship celebrations?

22. Y N   Do you send quarterly informational mailings to newcomers and others?

23. Y N   Do you schedule outreach Sundays to invite the larger community to join you in worship and fellowship?

24. Y N   Does a layperson make a follow-up contact within forty-eight hours to thank first-time visitors for attending the service?

25. Y N   Is a card or letter, over the pastor's signature, sent out to first-time visitors to thank them for attending the service?

26. Y N   Does a layperson make a follow-up contact within seven days to thank second- and third-time visitors for attending the service?

27. Y N   Does your telephone answering system give directions to the church, mention the hours of service and other opportunities, and say whether you have child care?

Total yes: _____ Total no: _____

Assess the Current Health of Your Welcoming System

Determine the level of health of the welcoming system using this chart:

27–21 yes answers: your system is optimally healthy.

20–16 yes answers: your system is generally healthy.

15–11 yes answers: your system needs strengthening.

10–6 yes answers: your system is unhealthy.

5–0 yes answers: your system is very unhealthy.

To make this system healthier, we recommend that you commit to implementing any twenty-one of the tactics in the WQ. The tactics you choose are simply ways for your church to adapt its welcoming system to improve current realities.

SURVEY TWO

Scan for Your Nurturing Quotient

Scan the current health of your nurturing system through this Nurturing Quotient (NQ) survey. Circle Y (yes) if you feel you implement an item or N (no) if you feel you do not. Not sure? Move on to the next one. List Y and N totals at the end of the survey.

1. Y N   Do you keep newcomer information and follow-ups in a database for additional contacts?
2. Y N   Do you have entry-level prayer groups for newcomers?
3. Y N   Do you have recovery groups or other support groups that meet at your church?
4. Y N   Do you offer entry-level short-term classes or workshops in which newcomers can participate?
5. Y N   Do you have social events at which newcomers feel they are welcome?
6. Y N   Do you sponsor community service activities in which newcomers can easily participate?
7. Y N   Do you have regularly scheduled newcomer orientation sessions (it could be a video) to introduce people to the life and work of the church?

(Continued)

Exhibit 7.2. Continued

8. Y N   Do you have classes for those interested in joining your
church?

9. Y N   Do you send quarterly mailings to visitors and others to keep
them apprised of church activities?

10. Y N   Do you have a new-member packet of information?

11. Y N   Are new members encouraged to participate in small groups
that have building relationships as their primary purpose?

12. Y N   Do you have trained prayer partners who are available for
newcomers' prayer requests and to pray with or for them?

13. Y N   Do you have a system through which members are placed in a
cluster of individuals who meet at least quarterly to plan events
and activities, enjoy fellowship, and get to know one another?

14. Y N   Do you provide a sponsor or mentor who is responsible for
easing a new member through the incorporation process?

15. Y N   Do you have a festive celebration when new members are
received into the fellowship of the church?

16. Y N   Do you have a centralized database for keeping accurate records
of member attendance and participation in the life of the church?

17. Y N   Do you monitor attendance so you can contact members
after they have missed three consecutive Sundays?

18. Y N   Do you use an intentional "greeting card ministry" for wed-
dings, anniversaries, birthdays, time of need or support, or
yearly anniversary of membership?

19. Y N   Do you provide ways to publicly celebrate and to be supportive of members' needs, joys, and concerns?

20. Y N   Do you have a system in place for ongoing telephone outreach?

21. Y N   Do you make attempts to get inactive members to return?

Total yes: _____ Total no: _____

Assessing Your Nurturing System's Current Level of Health

Now determine the level of health of your nurturing system using this chart.

21–17 yes answers: your system is optimally healthy.

16–14 yes answers: your system is generally healthy.

13–10 yes answers: your system needs strengthening.

9–6 yes answers: your system is unhealthy.

5–0 yes answers: your system is very unhealthy.

To make this system healthier, we recommend that you commit to implementing any seventeen of the tactics in the NQ. The tactics you choose are simply ways for your church to adapt its nurturing system to improve current realities.

SURVEY THREE

Scan for Your Empowering Quotient

Scan the current health of your empowering system through this Empowering Quotient (EQ) survey. Circle Y (yes) if you implement the item or N (no) if you do not. Not sure? Move on to the next item. List your Y and N totals at the end of this survey.

1. Y N   Are laity given responsibilities for "pastoral" care (caring, encouragement, support)?
2. Y N   Is training for volunteers provided regularly?
3. Y N   Is a person (or team) responsible for recruiting, training, and deploying volunteers?
4. Y N   Is a survey of spiritual gifts administered to all new (and long-term) members?
5. Y N   Do you have an interview process to connect people to possible ministry opportunities?
6. Y N   Do you sponsor a half-day or one-day workshop to explore ministry opportunities?
7. Y N   Do you provide written job descriptions for all volunteer opportunities?
8. Y N   Do you have short-term entry-level opportunities for ministry (less than a year)?
9. Y N   Do your volunteer projects have definite beginning and ending dates?
10. Y N   Do you publicly commission volunteers for lay ministry?
11. Y N   Is there a database system in place to indicate the passions, gifts, and skills of potential volunteers?

(Continued)

Exhibit 7.2. Continued

12. Y N   Do you have a formal way of debriefing by listening to the experiences and recommendations of volunteers?
13. Y N   Do you ask for a minimum commitment of time, talent, and treasure from new members?
14. Y N   Does your present system allow individual initiative in creating ministry opportunities not currently provided by the congregation?

       Total yes: _____ Total no: _____

Assessing Your Empowering System's Current Level of Health
Now determine the level of health of your empowering system using this chart.

    14–12 yes answers: your system is optimally healthy.
    11–9 yes answers: your system is generally healthy.
    8–6 yes answers: your system needs strengthening.
    5–3 yes answers: your system is unhealthy.
    2–0 yes answers: your system is very unhealthy.

To make this system healthier, we recommend that you commit to implementing any twelve of the tactics in the EQ. The tactics you choose are simply ways for your church to adapt its empowering system to improve current realities.

SURVEY FOUR

Scan for Your Serving Quotient
Scan the current health of your serving system through this Serving Quotient (SQ) survey. Circle Y (yes) if you implement the item or N (no) if you do not. Not sure? Move on to the next item. List your Y and N totals at the end of this survey.

1. Y N   Is there intentional small-group ministry in the congregation?
2. Y N   Are there written descriptions of each type of team or small group?
3. Y N   Do volunteer groups that serve others see themselves more as teams than as committees?

4. Y N Are there resource people to act as coaches for leaders of small groups?

5. Y N Does each small group or team know the specific way it carries out the mission of the congregation?

6. Y N Is each small group or team aware that it reflects the spiritual DNA or identity of the whole congregation?

7. Y N Are at least 40 percent of all groups in the congregation open to new people?

8. Y N Is there regularly scheduled ongoing training to support those serving in groups or teams?

9. Y N Do you replicate groups by creating new facilitators and team leaders?

10. Y N Do you have groups that replicate by intentionally multiplying and becoming two groups?

11. Y N Do you have groups that are intentional about inviting in newcomers?

12. Y N Do you send volunteers to conferences or workshops that focus on creating successful small-group ministry?

13. Y N Do you have established ways to recognize and thank leaders of small groups and teams?

14. Y N Do you debrief leaders of small groups and teams to assist you in strengthening the volunteer ministry?

Total yes: _____ Total no: _____

Assessing Your Serving System's Current Level of Health
Now determine the health of your serving system using this chart.

14–12 yes answers: your system is optimally healthy.
11–9 yes answers: your system is generally healthy.
8–6 yes answers: your system needs strengthening.
5–3 yes answers: your system is unhealthy.
2–0 yes answers: your system is very unhealthy.

To make this system healthier, we recommend that you commit to implementing any twelve of the tactics in the SQ. The tactics you choose are simply ways for your church to adapt its serving system to improve current realities.

Whom Shall We Serve?

That question in this sixth key step is the one that United Methodist lay-leader and conference official Paul Extrum-Fernandez feels is of utmost importance. He strongly supports using demographic and psychographic data because, as he says, "Before a congregation can get its 'market share,' it must learn all it can about the people it intends to serve."

Peter Drucker and Phillip Kotler address this issue in a dialogue in Drucker's *Managing the Non-Profit Organization*:

> DRUCKER: So, one of the first steps in marketing for the non-profit institution is to define its markets, its publics. Think through to whom you have to market your product and your strengths. That really comes before you think through the message, does it?
>
> KOTLER: Yes. Let's take churches, for example, because what you said poses a real problem for churches. On the one hand, a church should go after every person who wants a religious experience, and so on. It should therefore be a very diverse institution. On the other hand, marketing would suggest that it would be more successful if it defined its target group, whether it might be singles, divorced people, gay people, or whatever. How do you orchestrate very diverse groups and have a successful institution? That alone puts pressure on trying to define your market.

Targeting Your Audience

People are grouped by a variety of characteristics: age, sex, economics, attitude, values, lifestyle, or interests. These groups are "publics." Each is different from all others and has its own challenges; addressing each requires specific communication. Publics are both internal and external. *Internal publics* are those in the core group, the regular attenders, the occasional attenders, and of course newcomers who are seeking to move to the center of the life and work of the church.

External publics are potential participants who might be attracted to your congregation because of something you are doing but who are not currently involved with your faith community.

Targeting simply means making a decision as to those groups within the whole population, to whom and for whom and with whom you intend to provide ministry. Elsewhere in the Drucker-Kotler dialogue, Kotler says that a target audience is "not everyone; but it's more than one group. The church needs well-defined groups who are looking for one or more particular satisfactions."

Drucker adds, "So the mission may well be universal. And yet to be successful, the institution has to think through its strategy and focus on the main target groups in marketing and delivering its service."

How do you define your target audience? Market research can assist you. There are many good sources:

1. Your denomination

2. Your local chamber of commerce

3. Credit reporting agencies

4. Professional demographers, especially those interested in churches

Positioning: Windows in the Mind

Positioning is a term coined in 1972 by Al Ries and Jack Trout, two New York advertising executives who defined it as "an organized system for finding windows in the mind." Positioning, in a congregational sense, is communicating your unique strength to a targeted segment of the population so that they perceive your offer of transformation. Your target market is served well when you "listen to the customers" and discover their needs and wants; you discern that your congregation has the ability, the competence, and the passion necessary to serve your potential customers. Positioning is a crucial component because it defines your market niche—how you are unique, different from other congregations serving the same market. These differences might be music, drama or dance, creative educational programs for children, support groups for senior adults, charismatic preaching, healing, service to the community, or a host of other gifts.

There are three points to keep in mind as you position your congregation:

1. Determine what *positive* images already exist in the mind of your target publics about your congregation, and then reinforce them.

2. State, as simply as possible, who you are. The oversimplified message is the one that is heard, and it must be stated regularly, repeatedly, consistently, convincingly, and authentically. People want what is genuine, believable, and helpful.

3. To reach your target audience, use marketing methods that are *appropriate* for your congregation. You must be seen and heard where your audience is looking and listening. Those areas might include newspapers, newsletters, radio, television, direct mail in its many forms, and the Internet.

Example

First Church is located in an area that has recently begun to grow. Families with teenagers have moved into the area, yet the congregation is not attracting many young people to their teens program. So First Church determines to position itself in the mind of the target market (teens) by developing and communicating its offer of transformation. The church sponsors a listening time, when its own teenage members and their friends can describe what they are looking for from a church. What they hear is that these teens have two primary needs and wants. First, they would like regular time, one-on-one and in groups, with an adult who cares about and understands them, such as a mentor, tutor, or coach. Second, they want to serve the larger community through volunteer work. First Church takes a hard and realistic look at these needs and wants and decides yes, it has the desire and the resources to create and sponsor a mentoring program as well as a teen team that participates monthly in the ecumenical feeding program in the community.

Activity

Who are your target markets? Write a short description of them, and indicate why you believe your congregation has the ability and willingness to serve them.

Ministry Pathways: Broad Highways to the Future

A mind-set we often encounter focuses on the idea that there is a right way to God, that there is a ministry pathway to the kingdom of God that is the only legitimate way to "do church." We haven't yet found anyone who has identified it, but the belief is out there. We always remind those who hold this view that it isn't about doing church; it's about *being* church, in accordance with your spiritual DNA. This knowledge gives your congregation all that it needs to decide on appropriate ministry pathways or programs.

For the majority of congregations, a ministry pathway may be worship, education, spiritual formation, fellowship, relationship building, support, social action, or direct service to others. Congregations understand the importance of these pathways, but they often see them in the context of highly structured and independent programs, not in the organic sense. Any ministry pathway, to be effective, must reflect the spiritual DNA and be seen not as independent but *inter*dependent, contributing to the health and well-being of the congregation—the organism—as a whole. Consider three examples.

Spiritual Growth as a Ministry Pathway

More than fifty years ago, Gordon Cosby, an army chaplain and Baptist minister, envisioned a church that crossed all boundaries of race, economic status, and denomination, one that would serve the spiritual needs as well as the physical and emotional needs of those marginalized by society. Cosby also envisioned this church as a place where those who served others were themselves growing spiritually. Out of his vision was born the Church of the Saviour in Washington, D.C., and its associated faith communities. So effective is this church's model that it has been studied and used by hundreds of congregations throughout the country. Here is a church where the inward journey and the outward journey are one.

The Church of the Saviour understands that the primary need we all share is to find the presence of Christ within ourselves and others. They stand firm in the belief that the primary pathway to God for the congregation is to create a spiritual environment in which one can respond to God's call. Through worship and through mission groups that support change, the Church of the Saviour is a compelling example of just how effective ministry can be when it is based on the power that produces change.

Service to the Community as a Ministry Pathway

Glide Memorial Church is in the Tenderloin district of San Francisco, an ethnically diverse neighborhood where most of the city's homeless shelters and low-income housing are found. It's an area of rampant drug abuse and crime. Understandably, it's a place of despair for many. This locale would not be high on the list for church planners wanting to plant a thriving, growing congregation. Yet that's exactly what's happened. Without the external requirements for growth (such as adequate parking), and lacking an appropriate site in a safe area, Glide Church grew to almost ten thousand participants, first under Cecil Williams, and now under the leadership of Douglass Fitch.

How has this growth been possible? Glide clearly discerned that its primary pathway to spiritual transformation lay in direct service to the community. Today it sponsors more than forty service programs, including substance abuse recovery, job counseling, computer skills training, health care services, and a free feeding program that operates 365 days a year. Glide Memorial is powered by unconditional love and committed to community service as its central ministry pathway. Glide is an example that mission is much more powerful than location.

Education as a Ministry Pathway

The Forum at All Saints Church, Pasadena, California, is a large room with banked seating around four sides, inspired by the ancient forums of Rome and Greece. It is also a room shaped by the mind, a room that becomes a marketplace of ideas each Sunday morning. But it is most of all an expression of a commitment to education as an ongoing, lifelong adventure, a ministry pathway to transformation. The Forum meetings are held between worship services; they last from forty-five minutes to an hour. In that time, thousands have been "transformed by the renewing of their minds" (Romans 12:2 KJV). In this room some of the great minds of our time have explored significant issues and examined the moral and ethical aspects of those issues. Politicians and preachers, scientists and social activists, authors and teachers have all been drawn to this room. Poetic cadences have flowed from thinkers as diverse as Jesse Jackson, William Sloane Coffin, Matthew Fox, Walter Brueggemann, Desmond Tutu, and others. The speakers may not share a common religious perspective, but they all understand that transformation can come through sharing powerful ideas.

Activity

What are the three to five ministry pathways your congregation can offer with quality? Describe in what ways they reflect your spiritual DNA.

Your Goals and Objectives

Henry David Thoreau wrote, "If one advances confidently in the direction of his dreams, and endeavors to live the life which he has imagined, he will meet with a success unexpected in common hours. . . . Build your castles in the air, that is where they should be.

Now, put the foundations under them." Those "castles" are your hopes and dreams for the future, and your goals and objectives are the foundation.

Goals are overall outcomes you wish to achieve. They are part of the big picture as expressed through your vision. Goals left at the level of the desired state become nice but useless generalities. If they are to be actualized, they need something more: objectives.

Objectives are tied to goals; they make your goals concrete. They usually have three necessary qualities:

1. They are *specific* and are stated in clear terms.

2. They are *measurable*—that is, they indicate the success level desired.

3. They are *time-related*, stating when the objective will be achieved.

Let's consider two examples.

First, suppose your congregation's goal, as part of your vision for the future, is to increase the average Sunday attendance at the primary worship service. This is a fine goal; but unless objectives are added, it will probably not happen. So let's add an objective: the congregation wants to have at least two hundred people at the primary worship service by the first Sunday in June. This is specific, it's measurable, and it's time-related. Tactics, or action steps, can then be mapped as ways to assist the congregation in achieving its goal.

Or let's say you see quality education as part of your vision of a transformed world and you believe your congregation has the competence to offer this as a ministry pathway. Your objectives might look like this:

• Our congregation will have an adult forum that attracts an average of fifty adults by the end of January.

- We will offer in-depth classes for men about the convergence of religion and science during Lent of this year.

- Our congregation will offer five new study groups by Easter.

- We will offer quarterly workshops on parenting skills beginning in March.

Outline for Writing Your Strategic Map

We have witnessed the value of strategic mapping in hundreds of congregations as they encountered and embraced the challenges of contextual diversity and individual initiative. Strategic mapping generates strength not only to expect variations but to celebrate them. The outline in Exhibit 7.3 should help you create a strategic map for your congregation to see you through the changes that inevitably arise.

Final Thought

Is strategic mapping the solution to all the challenges facing mainline congregations today? No. But mapping can be a powerful tool if a congregation uses it as a way to describe its spiritual identity and the routes to transformation in the future. Moreover, because strategic mapping places such an emphasis on positive systemic changes, it assists a congregation in fulfilling the hope of Galatians 6: "Don't get tired of helping others. You will be rewarded when the time is right, if you don't give up."

Strategic mapping is a journey of faith that takes a congregation through unfamiliar yet compelling terrain. In this journey, there are unquestionably risks and tensions. But if a congregation holds fast to that which God has called it to become, it can renew, stretch, and grow.

Stay on the journey; the harvest is ready.

Exhibit 7.3. Outline of Strategic Map

STRATEGIC MAP OF (NAME OF CHURCH)

Preface
As part of your preface, provide an overview of the strategic mapping process, to empower those who did not participate.

Team Members
List the names of all those who participated.

_____

_____

Core Values
State and define those core values you chose during the process.

_____

_____

Mission Statement
State your mission (purpose) for being. The very heart of your mission is providing opportunities for the transformation of individuals and the community.

_____

_____

_____

_____

Vision Statement
State your vision—your "big picture," what you see God calling you to become. It entails out-picturing your values and implementing your mission.

_____

_____

_____

_____

_____

The Four Key Systems of the (Name of Church)
Briefly describe the four key systems. List the tactics you already have in place, then list those additional tactics you have chosen to make the systems healthier. We *strongly* recommend that you indicate who (team, staff, individual, and so on) is responsible for each tactic and by what date it is to be in place. For those tactics already in place and that are the responsibility of some person or group, please indicate the tactic, and who is responsible.

_____

_____

_____

_____

_____

_____

Ministry Teams: The Four-Team Approach
Ministry teams can be developed around each of the four systems to make sure the tactics are implemented. Create a ministry team for the four systems of your church. List each team and include the names of those who initially take responsibility for forming each ministry team.

Welcoming Team
This team carries out your mission by attracting and welcoming newcomers. The team's primary responsibility is to be welcoming to newcomers.
    Other responsibilities might include:

- Writing, designing, and printing a welcoming brochure
- Producing an annual Friendship Sunday
- Organizing a monthly newcomer orientation
- Following up on first-time, second-time, and third-time visitors
- Making sure that at least one growth group is available for newcomers after each attraction event

(Continued)

Exhibit 7.3. Continued

Nurturing Team

This ministry team carries out the mission by incorporating people into the body of Christ, providing opportunities for individuals to strengthen their faith and build stronger relationships. As we said earlier, data reveal that people need to make at least seven friends in six months to feel incorporated into the church. Here are examples of the responsibilities for this team:

- New-member brochure or materials
- New-member reception or celebration
- Mentor (or prayer partner) for each new member
- Newcomers or new-members class
- At least one growth group intended for incorporated people
- Other ministry activities (classes, workshops, social activities) offering the opportunity to build one's faith and to meet other incorporated people
- Special recognitions for birthdays, anniversaries, and so forth
- Spiritual direction
- Member directory or new-member pictures on bulletin board

Empowering Team

This team carries out the mission through recruiting, training, and deploying volunteers. The teams' responsibilities might include:

- A Ministry Fair or Vision Day, to share the church's spiritual DNA and to communicate volunteer opportunities that are available through the church
- Administering a spiritual gifts inventory to prospective volunteers
- One-on-one interview to discover the passions and discuss the gifts of a volunteer and to assist in discerning the volunteer's calling
- Designing and presenting a volunteer training (half-day, with food)
- Deployment, either by assigning the newly trained volunteer to an existing opportunity or explaining how he or she can create a new ministry activity
- Commissioning activities

Serving Team

This team serves newcomers, incorporated people, and the larger community through small groups and teams.

Responsibilities might include:

- Creating a nuclear leadership cell to explore how best to establish a small-group ministry
- Exploring additional training on small groups
- Coaching for leaders of small groups
- Monthly leadership meetings for support and training, and to facilitate replication of small groups
- Designing and being responsible for an annual recognition Sunday or recognition activity

_____

_____

Ministry Teams: The Single-Team Approach

Rather than four teams as listed above, some congregations prefer a single ministry team with responsibility for coordinating, initiating, and monitoring all tactics used to strengthen the systems.

_____

_____

Those Whom You Serve

The message of God's transforming love is for everyone. Realistically, however, you are particularly called to reach out to certain groups. List your target audience. Then, in a sentence or two, indicate why you have chosen to begin with these groups and what you feel you have to offer them. Describe how you intend to reach them.

_____

_____

(Continued)

Exhibit 7.3. Continued

Ministry Pathways
Connect your competencies and your passions with those whom you
serve by indicating programmatically the routes you'll take to your
congregation's vision. Typical pathways include worship, education,
fellowship, commitment to social justice, and so on. There are
commonly three to five broad pathways that a congregation can use
to offer transformation. Indicate the ministry pathways that are most
reflective of your spiritual DNA.

_____

_____

_____

Goals and Objectives
Goals and objectives give specificity to your vision. They also detail the
ministry pathways by furnishing elements of time and number. List the
major goals and objectives you are willing to commit to at this time.

_____

_____

_____

Resources

Richard Southern and Robert Norton
Church Development Systems
2269 Chestnut St., #621
San Francisco, CA 94123
415/878-2003; toll-free 888/801-1186
e-mail: cdsxroads@juno.com
(individual and cluster congregation consultations, workshops, facil-
itation of retreats, conference presentations)

Demographics

Claritas
5375 Mira Sorrento Pl.
San Diego, CA 92121
858/677-9650; toll-free 800/866-6510
(demographic information for United States and Canada)

The Percept Group
29889 Santa Margarita Pkwy.
Rancho Santa Margarita, CA 92688
949/635-1282; toll-free 800/442-6277

www.perceptnet.com
(demographic and psychographic information about the United States)

Yearbook of American and Canadian Churches
National Council of Churches
475 Riverside Dr., Rm. 850
New York, NY 10115
212/870-2227
www.electronicchurch.org
(basic information and statistics on mainstream and other American and Canadian denominations; issued yearly)

Organizations

Alban Institute
7315 Wisconsin Ave., Ste. 1250
West Bethesda, MD 20814
301/718-4407
www.alban.org
(books, materials, workshops, consultations, journal)

Church Innovations
1456 Branston St.
St. Paul, MN 55180
651/646-7633
www.churchinnovations.org
(small-group materials and videos)

Robert K. Greenleaf Center for Servant-Leadership
921 East 86th St., Ste. 200
Indianapolis, IN 46240
317/259-1241
www.greenleaf.org
(books, materials, and videos on servant-leadership)

Periodicals

Congregations, The Alban Journal
Alban Institute
7315 Wisconsin Ave., Ste. 1250
West Bethesda, MD 20814
301/718-4407
www.alban.org/periodicals.asp

Emerging Trends
Princeton Research Center
P.O. Box 389
Princeton, NJ 98542

Net Results
5001 Ave. N
Lubbock, TX 79412
806/762-8094
www.netresults.org

Religion Watch
P.O. Box 652
North Bellmore, NY 11710
www.religionwatch.com

Spiritual Gifts

"God's Special Gift for Me: A Study and Personal Evaluation of the
Nine Ministry-Oriented Spiritual Gifts" by Larry Gilbert
(child-friendly booklet includes scriptural passages on spiritual gifts)
Church Growth Institute
P.O. Box 7000
Forest, VA 24551
800/553-4769
www.churchgrowth.org

Find Your Fit: How Your Talents, Spiritual Gifts and Personality Add Up to You by Jane Kise and Kevin Johnson
Bethany House Publishers
11400 Hampshire Avenue So.
Minneapolis, MN 55438
800/328-6109
www.bethanyhouse.com

LifeKeys, Discovering Who You Are, Why You're Here and What You Do Best by David Stark, Sandra Hirsch, and Jane Kise
Bethany House Publishers
11400 Hampshire Avenue So.
Minneapolis, MN 55438
800/328-6109
www.bethanyhouse.com

"Houts Inventory of Spiritual Gifts" and "Trenton Spiritual Gifts Analysis"
Leadership Centre
P.O. Box 41083 RPO South
Winfield, B.C., Canada V4V 1Z7
800/804-0777

"Spiritual Gifts Survey"
by Calvie Hughson Schwalm
Crystal Cathedral
13280 Chapman Ave.
Garden Grove, CA 92840
714/971-4000

Bibliography

Adams, J. R. *So You Can't Stand Evangelism? A Thinking Person's Guide to Church Growth*. Cambridge, Mass.: Cowley, 1994.

Arn, W. *The Church Growth Ratio Book*. Monrovia, Calif.: Church Growth, 1990.

Artress, L. In *Source* (Grace Cathedral, San Francisco), Fall 1999.

Bandy, T. G. *Moving Off the Map: A Field Guide to Changing the Congregation*. Nashville: Abingdon Press, 1998.

Bandy, T. G. *Christian Chaos: Revolutionizing the Congregation*. Nashville: Abingdon Press, 1999.

Banks, R., and Stevens, P. *The Complete Book of Everyday Christianity*. Downers Grove, Ill.: Intervarsity Press, 1997.

Barker, J. A. *Paradigms: The Business of Discovering the Future*. New York: HarperBusiness, 1992.

Barna, G. *Re-Churching the Unchurched*. Ventura, Calif.: Issachar Resources, 2000.

Bass, D. C. (ed.). *Practicing Our Faith: A Way of Life for a Searching People*. San Francisco: Jossey-Bass, 1997.

Bauknight, B. K. *Body Building: Creating a Ministry Team Through Spiritual Gifts*. Nashville: Abingdon Press, 1996.

Beaudoin, T. *Virtual Faith: The Irreverent Spiritual Quest of Generation X*. San Francisco: Jossey-Bass, 1998.

Bennis, W. "The Secrets of Great Groups." In F. Hesselbein and P. M. Cohen (eds.), *Leader to Leader: Enduring Insights on Leadership*. San Francisco: Jossey-Bass, 1999.

Braden, S. *The First Year: Incorporating New Members*. Nashville: Discipleship Resources, 1987.

Brussat, F., and Brussat, M. A. *Spiritual Literacy: Reading the Sacred in Everyday Life*. New York: Simon & Schuster, 1998.

Cimino, R. (ed.). *Religion Watch*, April 1999.

Cousins, D., Anderson, L., and DeKruyter, A. *Mastering Church Management.* Portland, Oreg.: Multnomah Press, 1990.

Davis, W. L. "Evangelizing the Pre-Christian Male," *Net Results*, June 2001.

De Mello, A. *Awakening: The Perils and Opportunities of Reality.* New York: Bantam Doubleday, 1990.

Drucker, P. *Managing the Non-Profit Organization: Principles and Practice.* New York: HarperCollins, 1990.

Easum, W. M. *Sacred Cows Make Gourmet Burgers.* Nashville: Abingdon Press, 1995.

Fincke, R., and Stark, R. *The Churching of America 1776–1990.* Rutgers, N.J.: Rutgers University Press, 1992.

Forman, R. "Report of Grassroots Spirituality." Cited in K. Wilber, *One Taste: The Journals of Ken Wilber.* Boston: Shambala, 1999.

George, C. *Prepare Your Church for the Future.* Tarrytown, N.Y.: Fleming H. Revell, 1991.

Goa, D. J., Distad, L., and Wangler, M. *Anno Domini: Jesus Through the Centuries—Exploring the Heart of Two Millennia.* Gallery Guide. Edmonton, Alberta, Canada: Provincial Museum, 2000.

Greenleaf, R. K. *Servant Leadership: A Journey into the Nature of Legitimate Power and Greatness.* Mahwah, N.J.: Paulist Press, 1977.

Greenleaf, R. K. *The Servant as Leader.* Indianapolis, Ind.: Robert K. Greenleaf Center, 1991.

Grinnell, J. In *Business Leader*, Sept. 1996.

Hadaway, C. K., and Roozen, D. A. *Rerouting the Protestant Mainstream.* Nashville: Abingdon Press, 1995.

Hargrove, R. *Masterful Coaching Fieldbook.* San Francisco: Jossey-Bass Pfeiffer, 2000.

Hauck, K. C. *Antagonists in the Church: How to Identify and Deal with Destructive Conflict.* Minneapolis: Augsburg Fortress, 1988.

Herrington, J., Bonem, M., and Furr, J. H. *Leading Congregational Change: A Practical Guide for the Transformational Journey.* San Francisco: Jossey-Bass, 2000.

Houts, R. "Houts Inventory of Spiritual Gifts." South Winfield, B.C., Canada: International Centre for Leadership Development and Evangelism.

Huxley, A. *After Many a Summer Dies the Swan.* Chicago: Elephant, 1993.

Jones, L. B. *Jesus, CEO: Using Ancient Wisdom for Visionary Leadership.* New York: Hyperion, 1995.

Katzenbach, J., and Smith, D. *The Wisdom of Teams.* New York: HarperCollins, 1931.

Kew, R., and White, R. *Toward 2015: A Church Odyssey*. Cambridge, Mass.:
    Cowley, 1997.

Mead, L. *The Once and Future Church*. New York: Alban Institute, 1992.

Morris, M. *Volunteer Ministries: New Strategies for Today's Church*. Sherman, Tex.:
    Newton-Cline Press, 1990.

Morrissey, M. M. *A Miracle in Motion*. Wilsonville, Oreg.: Tiger Mountain Press,
    1995.

Niebuhr, G. "American Religion at the Millennium's End." In *Yearbook of Amer-
    ican and Canadian Churches 1999*. New York: National Council of the
    Churches of Christ, 1999.

Nouwen, H. *Reaching Out: Three Movements of the Spiritual Life*. New York: Dou-
    bleday, 1986.

O'Connor, E. *Call to Commitment: An Attempt to Embody the Essence of the
    Church*. Washington, D.C.: Servant Leadership Press, 1994.

Palmer, P. J. *Leading from Within: Reflections of Spirituality and Leadership*. Indi-
    anapolis: Indiana Office for Campus Ministries, 1990.

Putnam, R. D. *Bowling Alone: The Collapse and Revival of American Community*.
    New York: Simon and Schuster, 2000.

Ray, P. "The Rise of Integral Culture." Cited in K. Wilber, *One Taste: The Jour-
    nals of Ken Wilber*. Boston: Shambala, 1999.

Ries, A., and Trout, J. *Positioning: The Battle for Your Mind*. New York: Warner, 1986.

Roof, W. C. In *Christian Century*, Oct. 11, 2000, p. 993.

Savage, J. In W. D. Hendricks, *Exit Interviews*. Chicago: Moody Press, 1993.

Schramm, M. *Gifts of Grace*. Minneapolis: Augsburg, 1982.

Senge, P. *The Dance of Change: The Challenge to Sustaining Momentum in Learning
    Organizations*. New York: Doubleday, 1999.

Shea, J. In F. and M. A. Brussat, *Spiritual Literacy: Reading the Sacred in Everyday
    Life*. New York: Simon and Schuster, 1998.

Steindel-Rast, D. *Gratefulness, the Heart of Prayer: An Approach to Life in Full-
    ness*. Ramsey, N.J.: Paulist Press, 1984.

Steinke, P. L. *Healthy Congregations: A Systems Approach*. New York: Alban
    Institute, 1996.

Sweet, L. *11 Genetic Gateways to Spiritual Awakening*. Nashville: Abingdon
    Press, 1998.

Trueblood, D. E. *A Life of Search*. Richmond, Ind.: Friends United Press, 1996.

Tully, B. In C. Trueheart "Welcome to the Next Church." *Atlantic Monthly*,
    August 1996.

Ware, C. *Discover Your Spiritual Type: A Guide to Individual and Congregational
    Growth*. New York: Alban Institute, 1995.

Ware, C. *Connecting to God: Nurturing Spirituality Through Small Groups*. New York: Alban Institute, 1997.

Warren, R. *The Purpose-Driven Church: Growth Without Compromising Your Message and Mission*. Grand Rapids, Mich.: Zondervan, 1995.

Weams, L. *Church Leadership*. Quoted in S. Rehnborg, *The Starter Kit for Mobilizing Ministry*. Tyler, Tex.: Leadership Network, 1994.

Wheatley, M. *Leadership and the New Science: Learning About Organization from an Orderly Universe*. San Francisco: Berrett-Koehler, 1994.

Wilber, K. *One Taste: The Journals of Ken Wilber*. Boston: Shambala, 1999.

Williamson, T. P. *Attending Parishioners' Spiritual Growth*. New York: Alban Institute, 1997.

Wilson, M. *How to Mobilize Church Volunteers*. Minneapolis: Augsburg Fortress, 1983.

Wise, S. In F. and M. A. Brussart, *Spiritual Literacy: Reading the Sacred in Everyday Life*. New York: Simon & Schuster, 1998.

Wuthnow, R. *Sharing the Journey: Support Groups and America's New Quest for Community*. New York: Free Press, 1994.

Young, D. S. *Servant Leadership for Church Renewal*. Scottdale, Pa.: Herald Press, 1999.

Index

Page numbers in italic denote exhibits.